It's You vs You

Unleash Your Power,
Conquer Your Inner Battles
&
Transform Your Life

It's You vs You

Unleash Your Power,
Conquer Your Inner Battles
&
Transform Your Life

Riya Nandagawali

Highbrow Scribes Publications
New Delhi

It's You vs You
Riya Nandagawali

Published 2025 by Highbrow Scribes Publications

Printed in New Delhi, India

ISBN: 978-81-980325-1-5

Highbrow Scribes Publications's mission is to foster a universal
passion for reading by partnering with authors to help create stories
and communicate ideas that inform, entertain, and inspire, and to
connect them with readers everywhere.

Highbrow Scribes Publications books are printed on acid-free paper.

www.highbrowscribes.com

Dedicated to
My mother, Varsha

Your strength, resilience and unwavering determination have been my greatest inspiration

Contents

PART THREE : Mental and Physical Well-being

PART FOUR : Taking Actions and Responsibilities

Epigraph

Life is all about the way you respond or react in any situation which can shape the outcome significantly. Our reactions determine the narrative we create in our interactions.

Varsha M.N.

Author's Note

Dear Readers,

As you embark on this journey through *It's You vs You*, I want to take a moment to share why I felt compelled to write this book.

In a world filled with external pressures and expectations, we often find ourselves in a battle against our own limiting beliefs, fears and self-doubts. This book is a reflection of my own journey, one that has taught me that the most significant challenges we face are often within us.

My hope is to empower you to recognise that you are your own greatest obstacle and your own greatest ally. Each chapter is designed to guide you in identifying and overcoming the beliefs that hold you back, fostering self-awareness, ultimately leading to personal growth.

I believe that everyone has the potential to create a life they love but it requires the courage to confront the barriers we impose on ourselves. This book is not just about self-help; it's about self-discovery, resilience and the transformative power of mindset.

Together, we will explore practical strategies and real-life examples that illustrate how you can shift from reacting to responding, embrace your true potential and love life to the fullest.

Thank you for taking this journey with me. I hope you find inspiration, insight and the tools you need to turn the tide in your own life.

Here's to conquering the battle within!

Warm regards,
Riya M. N.

Preface

In the quiet corners of every mind, a battle rages—a relentless struggle between who we are and who we could be. We often seek external enemies, distractions that mask the truth: our greatest opponent resides within.

It's the struggle between the person you are today and the person you're capable of becoming. It's the clash between your fears and your potential, your doubts and your dreams.

For every step forward, there's a voice whispering 'you can't'. For every triumph, there's a shadow of self-doubt lurking. But what if you could silence that voice? What if you could harness your inner strength to overcome the obstacle holding you back?

The truth is—you are your own greatest adversary. And you are your own most powerful ally.

This book is an invitation to join the most important fight of your life—the fight against the limitations you've imposed on yourself. It's time to confront the enemy within and emerge victorious.

Acknowledgements

Writing this book has been an incredible journey and I would like to take a moment to express my gratitude to those who have supported me along the way.

First and foremost, I am grateful to my family and friends for their unwavering encouragement and belief in me. Your support has been a source of strength.

I would like to extend my heartfelt gratitude to my editor and literary agent, Jasmeet Walia, the brilliant founder of Fusion Lit. Her expertise and guidance have been invaluable throughout the writing process of this book. Jasmeet, your dedication to refining every word and ensuring clarity and flow has truly made a difference. This book wouldn't have been the same without your contributions, and for that, I am deeply thankful.

I am truly grateful to Vandana Bhatia Palli and the entire team at Highbrow Scribes Publications for their support and dedication throughout the journey of bringing this book to life. Their professionalism, expertise and commitment have been invaluable, and I am truly thankful for their belief in this project. Working with such a talented team has been a privilege, and I am deeply appreciative of their guidance and collaboration.

To my readers, thank you for embarking on this journey of self-discovery and transformation with me. Your willingness to confront your fears and embrace growth is what makes this work meaningful. I hope the lessons and strategies shared in this book empower you to take change in your life and break through the barriers that hold you back.

Finally, a special vote of thanks to everyone who shared their personal stories with me. Your courage in opening up about your struggles and triumphs has enriched this work profoundly. It is a testament to our shared humanity and the strength we gain from our experiences. Together, let us continue to challenge ourselves, uplift one another and strive toward realising our fullest potential.

Introduction

If you've read my debut book, *You Are the Best Father*, you're already familiar with some of the challenges I've faced. In that book, I shared the obstacles my family encountered and the lessons I learned from my parents about resilience and positivity.

Growing up, I was always a carefree girl, living life without a worry in the world. But the day I lost my pillar of strength—my father—I felt like I had fallen from the seventh cloud. It was as if my world had crumbled beneath me. From that moment onwards, every struggle and every challenge I faced, shaped me into a stronger person. Yes, I went through the worst phases; moments that broke me down and left me deeply uncomfortable. Today, when I look back, I realise that those were the moments that pushed me to grow.

I've now reached a point in my life where I no longer see challenges as problems. I've learned that what we often label as "problems" are in reality full of opportunities—chances to grow, evolve and prove our resilience. It's all about how we choose to tackle them and make our lives worthwhile.

As a psychologist, I've worked with many people who face their own inner battles and I genuinely want to help others find their way through mental health struggles. That's why I wrote *It's You vs You*—to share my journey and provide you with insights and tools to enrich your life and find fulfilment. This book will show you how to face challenges head-on, build mental strength and unlock your full potential.

This book is divided into four parts.

Part One is about self-awareness, focusing on identifying your strengths and weaknesses and how to develop a growth mindset.

Part Two talks about discipline, setting goals and following a regular regime. Once this is incorporated, you shall then learn how to overcome any distractions and track your progress.

Part Three puts emphasis on your mental and physical well-being. Here, you shall learn how to overcome self-doubt and overthinking, and ultimately, lead a healthy life with a strong mind and peace.

Part Four concludes with taking actions and responsibilities. By the time you finish reading this book, you shall learn how to break free from the cocoon of the comfort zone, learn from failures and walk towards the path of success.

Ultimately, this self-help book is not just about finding motivation or inspiration; it's about shifting the mindset from one of victimhood to one of empowerment. Life is full of challenges, but it's how you respond to those challenges that defines your journey. Every day, you are faced with choices that can either move you closer to your goals or hold you back. The author wants readers to realise that they are in the driver's seat. You can choose to steer your life in the direction of your dreams, or you can choose to drift aimlessly. But the choice, and the responsibility, is always yours.

It's You vs You is a call to action for anyone feeling stuck, overwhelmed, or discouraged. It's a reminder that no matter how big the problem may seem, the solution starts with you. By embracing this mindset, you can unlock your full potential and create the life you've always wanted. The power to change your life is within your control—it always has been and always will be. And once you realise that, you become—unstoppable.

The Mirror Exercise

Have you ever stood in front of the mirror and admired your raw reflection? Forget about your external getup for a while. Just stand before the mirror and look into your eyes.

Who did you see?

A Champion or a critic?

A Dreamer or a doubter?

A Warrior or a worrier?

The reflection staring back at you holds the key to unlocking your true potential. Then what is weighing you down? Look at your reflection carefully and be honest with yourself. Yes, you can now see your deepest fears and insecurities.

Do not panic. Just sit back and relax. You are not alone. I am there with you. This book is about confronting that reflection, embracing your flaws and unleashing your inner strength. It's about recognising that the greatest opponent you'll ever face is the person you are today.

It's YOU vs YOU. The battle begins now!

Your Mind is a Battlefield

"The mind is a battlefield where your thoughts can either be your greatest weapon or your fiercest enemy."

The greatest battle we face is not against *external* forces but against our own minds. It's the struggle to overcome self-doubt, fear and pessimism. This internal conflict can either hold us back or propel us forward. So how can you win this inner battle? Just three tactics—Self awareness, courage and determination.

Who are those inner demons—our formidable foes—that have obstructed your paths? Let's look at those six creepers and what they denote.

1. Self-doubt: I'm not good enough

2. Fear: I'll never succeed

3. Negativity: I can't do this

4. Procrastination: I'll do it tomorrow

5. Excuses: I don't have enough resources

6. Overthinking: I need to think about it

These thoughts can cripple our potential but recognising them is the first step to victory.

The mind is the arena where this battle rages depending upon the three parameters as below:

1. Thoughts: Positive or negative, they shape our reality.

2. Emotions: Fear, anxiety or courage, they fuel our actions.

3. Actions: Our choices reflect our inner state

The mind as a battlefield illustrates the constant struggle between various thoughts, emotions and beliefs that shape our perceptions and actions. By mastering your thoughts and emotions, you can influence your decisions, reactions and ultimately the direction of your life. When you cultivate a disciplined and focused mindset, you can navigate challenges more effectively and pursue your goals with greater clarity and determination.

Your mind is the ultimate battlefield, where thoughts, emotions and beliefs clash. This internal struggle can either empower or ensnare you.

Your mind is both your greatest ally and your fiercest opponent. It has the power to build, to create, to inspire—but it can also destroy, sabotage and hold you captive. The difference lies in how well you understand this battlefield and how ready you are to fight the battles that arise within.

This book is your guide to recognising the forces at play inside your mind and to stepping into the role of your own commander. It's not about avoiding conflict or silencing self-doubt altogether. It's about transforming those challenges into a source of resilience, about embracing each struggle as an opportunity to become stronger, wiser and truer to yourself.

So, as you flip through these pages, know that you are not alone in this journey. The battle may be difficult, but it is one worth fighting. And through it all, you'll find that the most important victory you'll ever achieve is the one over your own mind.

Prepare to step onto the battlefield—and discover the strength that's always been within you.

"If you can control your mind, you can control your destiny."

PART ONE

Self-Awareness

1

The Strength of Self-Awareness

"Knowing yourself is the beginning of all wisdom"

~ Aristotle

Rishi had a promising career in a large corporation. He worked hard with utmost dedication but felt something was missing. Although he pushed himself every day, his achievements rarely brought him satisfaction. Whenever he faced setbacks, he would blame others—his team, the manager or his bad luck.

Rishi's relationships suffered too. He struggled to understand why people distanced themselves from him or why he often felt misunderstood. He believed everyone around him was flawed, and that if they changed, his life would be better. However, he never stopped to ask himself why he felt so unsatisfied or what he could change within himself to improve his life.

Years passed and Rishi remained stuck in this loop of frustration. He switched jobs frequently, hoping each new environment would bring him happiness, but the result was always the same. Without the ability to reflect and understand himself, he couldn't see that his own lack of awareness was at the root of his unhappiness.

Over time, Rishi's career stagnated, and he found himself feeling disconnected and bitter, unable to realise that his life could change if he simply looked inward. If only he could understand that he lacked self-awareness, life would have been a pleasant journey for him.

What is Self-awareness?

Self-awareness is the ability to recognise and understand your own thoughts, emotions, motivations and behaviours. It is a fundamental aspect of personal growth and a crucial tool in your journey. By becoming self-aware, you gain insights into your inner workings which enables you to navigate life's challenges more effectively and make choices that align with your true self.

Now, let's see another example.

Vamika was a young professional with high ambitions and a desire to make an impact. Unlike Rishi, she was deeply in touch with her strengths, weaknesses and values. She regularly took time to reflect, asking herself questions like:

- What motivates me?

- What makes me anxious?

- How can I grow?

At work, Vamika faced challenges too, but instead of blaming her surroundings, she took each setback as a chance to grow. When she received critical feedback, she paused, reflected and asked herself how she could use it constructively. This self-awareness helped her continuously improve and she quickly became a respected and trusted team member.

In her personal life, Vamika's relationships flourished because she was mindful of her actions and understood how her behaviour affected others. She took responsibility for her mistakes and learned from them, allowing her to build meaningful connections.

Through self-awareness, Vamika created a life of purpose and fulfilment. She faced challenges with resilience, learned from each experience and constantly evolved. Her story shows how, with self-awareness, we can achieve growth, fulfilment and a deeper understanding of ourselves.

Why does Self-awareness Matter?

- **Foundation of Personal Growth:** Without understanding who you are and what drives you, it's challenging to set goals or pursue growth effectively.

- **Improved Decision-Making:** When you are aware of your values and motivations, you can make choices that align with your true self. This leads to more authentic and fulfilling decisions.

- **Enhanced Relationships:** Understanding your emotions and behaviours helps you communicate better and empathise with others, fostering deeper and more meaningful connections.

- **Emotional Regulation:** Self-awareness allows you to identify and understand your emotions, enabling you to manage them more effectively. This leads to reduced stress and improved mental well-being.

- **Increased Resilience:** When you are aware of your strengths and weaknesses, you can build resilience against life's challenges. This awareness helps you adapt and thrive in difficult situations.

How to Develop Self-awareness?

There are three effective ways in which you can channelise yourself to develop self-awareness.

1. Reflective Journaling

2. Mindfulness and Meditation

3. Self-Reflection

Reflective Journaling

During your school or college days you would often carry a personal notebook which was your confidant. You would either scribble your thoughts or make it a routine to pen down your daily or significant experiences. This is called journaling. Unknown to you, it was a good habit. If you still maintain a secret diary then I pat you on your back. If you have stopped doing it then restart this endeavour. If you haven't ever done it then retrieve a notebook and a pen.

So, as a novice, how shall you begin?

1. **Set Aside Time:** Dedicate a specific time each day or week for journaling.

2. **Use Prompts:** If you're unsure where to start, consider prompts such as:

   - What am I feeling right now and why?

   - What thoughts have dominated my mind lately?

   - What are my core values and how do they influence my decisions?

3. **Reflect on Experiences:** After significant events, reflect on your thoughts and feelings.

- What did you learn about yourself?

- Are you happy or still learning?

- Are you able to sense significant changes within you?

Mindfulness and Meditation

Practising mindfulness involves staying fully present in the moment, paying attention to your thoughts, emotions and surroundings without judgement. It helps reduce stress, improve focus and enhance emotional well-being by encouraging awareness and acceptance of the present experience.

Meditation involves focusing the mind on a specific object, thought or activity such as breathing while letting go of distractions. It promotes relaxation, mental clarity and inner peace, helping to reduce stress and improve emotional regulation.

Self-Reflection

Taking time for self-reflection is crucial for developing self-awareness. This practice allows you to consider your thoughts, feelings and actions critically.

Let's look at some steps for effective self-reflection:

- Find a peaceful environment where you can reflect on yourself without distractions

- Note down what you have learnt throughout the week

- Identify the different challenges you have handled

and what would have been the better way to overcome them

- Focus on your goals and seek out ways to achieve them

Honesty is a non-negotiable attribute. Approach self-reflection with honesty and compassion. Acknowledge both your strengths and areas for improvement.

Overcoming Barriers to Self-awareness

While developing self-awareness is essential, various barriers can hinder your progress. Identifying and addressing these obstacles is crucial for deepening your self-understanding.

What are the Common Barriers to Self-awareness?

1. **Fear of Confrontation:** Many individuals fear facing uncomfortable truths about themselves. Acknowledging weaknesses or past mistakes can be daunting but is essential for growth.

2. **Defensiveness:** When receiving feedback, defensiveness can prevent you from truly hearing others' perspectives. Practise active listening and remain open to constructive criticism.

3. **Busy Lifestyle:** In the hustle and bustle of daily life, it's easy to overlook the importance of self-reflection. Prioritise time for introspection even if it means carving out just a few minutes each day.

4. **Negative Self-Talk:** Inner critics often undermine self-awareness by fostering self-doubt. Challenge negative thoughts by focusing on your achievements and strengths.

Accepting Inner Clarity

In a world that often pulls us in countless directions, self-awareness emerges as a beacon of clarity and strength. It empowers us to understand our thoughts, emotions and motivations, enabling us to navigate life's challenges with greater resilience and purpose. We unlock the potential to transform our relationships, make more informed decisions and cultivate a deeper connection with our true selves. As we embark on this journey of self-discovery, we learn to accept our imperfections and celebrate our unique strengths. Ultimately, self-awareness is not just a tool for personal growth; it is the foundation upon which we build a fulfilling and meaningful life, guiding us toward authenticity, compassion and profound inner peace. Embrace this power and watch as it illuminates your path to becoming the best version of yourself.

Self-awareness allows us to see ourselves clearly, but it also reveals the deeper layers of our mindset, where limiting beliefs often reside.

When we become more aware of our patterns, behaviours and reactions, we may notice that many of them are influenced by invisible forces—beliefs we've unknowingly accepted over time. These beliefs often hold us back, keeping us from fully embracing our potential.

"Through silence, we uncover the soul's true voice.

In knowing ourselves, we reclaim our choice."

2

Identifying Limiting Beliefs

"The only thing standing between you and your goal is the story you keep telling yourself as to why you can't achieve it."

Now that we've cultivated the power of self-awareness, we can begin the deeper work of uncovering the beliefs that influence our lives—often without us even realising it. These beliefs, formed by past experiences, societal expectations and internalised fears, can either empower us to grow or hold us back from achieving our true potential.

Limiting beliefs are often subtle, hidden in the background of our daily thoughts and decisions, yet they shape the way we see ourselves and the world around us. They may have been ingrained in us over time, influencing how we handle challenges, view our capabilities and interact with others.

In the journey of personal growth, identifying limiting beliefs are often deeply ingrained and can silently dictate your choices, actions and overall perception of ourselves and the world. They can serve as invisible barriers, hindering your progress and keeping us confined to a reality far below our potential. Limiting beliefs are often deeply rooted assumptions that arise from past experiences, cultural conditioning or negative feedback from others.

Recognising Your Own Limiting Beliefs

To identify your limiting beliefs, take time for reflection. Ask yourself questions like:

- What fears hold me back from pursuing my dreams?

- Are there patterns in my life where I feel stuck?

- What negative beliefs about myself do I repeat?

Once you've identified a belief, challenge it. And ask yourself:

- Is this belief based on facts or assumptions?

- What evidence do I have that contradicts this belief?

- How would my life change if I let go of this belief?

Transforming Limiting Beliefs

Identify and challenge negative thoughts, reframing them into positive affirmations. This practice not only helps to rewire your mindset but also encourages you to take actionable steps towards your goals. As you challenge and change these beliefs, you'll begin to notice a shift in your perspective, opening doors to new possibilities and opportunities.

Addressing limiting beliefs is a powerful act of self-awareness and self-love. As you confront these beliefs, you are taking a crucial step in reclaiming your power.

Embrace the idea that you have the ability to rewrite your story.

Remember, the journey begins with awareness and the commitment to change. Let's read the story of Ayush.

Ayush had always dreamt of becoming an entrepreneur. He was creative, driven and had a strong passion for technology. But for years, despite his ambition, he remained stuck in a corporate job he disliked. Every time he thought about launching his own business, a nagging voice inside his head would stop him:

- You're not good enough.

- You don't have the experience.

- What if you fail?

For Ayush, these thoughts were more than just fleeting worries—they were deeply ingrained beliefs that shaped his actions (or lack thereof). He had always been taught that security was the key to happiness. His parents, well-meaning but cautious, had instilled in him the belief that success came from climbing the corporate ladder, not from taking risks. The idea of entrepreneurship seemed far too uncertain, and so, Ayush stayed in his safe, predictable job.

But one day, while attending a seminar on personal growth, Ayush had a moment of clarity. The speaker discussed the concept of limiting beliefs—the internal narratives that hold us back, often without us realising it. As the speaker spoke about the ways in which these beliefs are formed, Ayush began to recognise that his fears and hesitations were based on beliefs that didn't serve him anymore. He was living according to someone else's blueprint for success.

Later that evening, Ayush took some time to reflect. He asked himself some tough questions:

- Why do I believe I'm not good enough to be an entrepreneur?

- What if my past failures don't define my future?

- What if I could find a way to take small risks that build my confidence?

As he delved deeper into these questions, he uncovered something powerful. His limiting beliefs were rooted in fear—fear of failure, fear of rejection and the belief that he wasn't capable of handling the unpredictability of entrepreneurship. These beliefs had been shaped by his upbringing, societal expectations and his own past experiences, particularly the times he had tried and failed in small business ventures during his younger years.

The most surprising revelation for Ayush, however, was this: these beliefs were not the truth. They were just stories he had told himself for so long that he had come to believe them as facts. And once he realised that these beliefs were not fixed truths, the weight they carried began to lighten.

Ayush decided to confront his limiting beliefs head-on. He started by reframing his thoughts. Instead of saying, "I'm not good enough to start a business", he told himself, "I have the skills and resources to make this work." Instead of focusing on the possibility of failure, he shifted his focus to what he could learn from any challenges that came his way.

He began by setting small, manageable goals: researching the industry, testing his ideas with a small group of people and slowly building a network of like-minded entrepreneurs. With each small step, Ayush built confidence and his limiting beliefs began to lose their power.

A year later, Ayush had launched his own tech startup.

It wasn't a huge success overnight, but it was enough for him to prove to himself that his limiting beliefs were, in fact, the only thing holding him back. With his business steadily growing, Ayush now felt more fulfilled and aligned with his true purpose. The fears he once had no longer controlled him, because he had recognised them for what they were—stories that had been crafted from doubt and fear, not fact or truth.

Limiting Beliefs are not Facts

The beliefs that hold us back are often based on past experiences, societal expectations or fears that we carry with us from childhood. But once we begin to question these beliefs—asking ourselves if they are truly valid—we open the door to transformation.

Recognising your limiting beliefs is the first step to breaking free from them. When we challenge the negative stories we've been telling ourselves, we take back our power and give ourselves permission to grow beyond what we thought was possible.

So, ask yourself:

- What beliefs are holding me back from reaching my full potential?

- Are they really true or are they just stories I've accepted as facts?

Once you start questioning these beliefs, you'll be amazed at how many of them simply dissolve, making way for a new and improved version of yourself.

In the quiet corners of the mind,
Whispers of fear, the ties that bind,
"Not enough. Too late," they softly say,
Building walls that lead us astray.

But shine a light on those shadows deep,
Question the thoughts that steal our sleep.
What if we dared to rise and see,
The power within, the chance to be free?

Unravel the stories that hold you back,
Rewrite the script, find your own track.
With each revelation, let courage ignite,
Transform limiting beliefs into wings of flight.

3

Exploring Strength and Weaknesses

"True strength is found in the courage to face your weaknesses and grow from them."

In the journey of personal growth, one of the most valuable steps is understanding our strengths and weaknesses. Knowing these aspects of ourselves brings clarity to who we are, what we want and how we can best navigate life's challenges.

Strength and weakness are often seen as polar opposites, yet both play essential roles in shaping our identity and pushing us toward self-improvement.

So, how important is it to understand both our strengths and weaknesses?

It's natural to focus on our strengths. They give us confidence and fuel our ambitions. But it's equally important to acknowledge and accept our weaknesses. Often, we tend to shy away from them, viewing them as flaws or failures. However, acknowledging your weaknesses doesn't make you weak—it makes you aware. And that awareness is the first step toward improving yourself.

Recognising both your strengths and weaknesses allows you to make better decisions, communicate more effectively and align your actions with your true potential. It's about balance—using your strengths to propel you forward while working on your weaknesses without letting them define you.

Here is a story about Sarah that shall help you to understand the concept better.

Sarah, a talented graphic designer, had always been praised for her creativity and attention to detail. Her strengths were evident in her work—she had an innate ability to think outside the box and bring fresh ideas to life. Colleagues often turned to her for innovative solutions and clients loved the unique touch she added to every project.

However, Sarah had a weakness that she had long ignored: a tendency to procrastinate. She often left tasks until the last minute, which resulted in unnecessary stress and sometimes, subpar work. Deep down, Sarah knew this was a weakness but she convinced herself it wasn't a big deal. She thought, "I can still meet deadlines and my work is good enough."

However, over time, the pressure of her procrastination started to affect her health and relationships. She realised that in trying to ignore her weakness, she was allowing it to hold her back.

One day, Sarah had a conversation with her mentor who asked her a simple question: "What's holding you back from being your best self?"

The question struck a chord with Sarah. She had never truly examined her procrastination or how it impacted her overall performance and well-being. She had been so focused on her strengths that she neglected to face the reality of her weaknesses.

After reflecting on the question, Sarah realised that procrastination was not just about poor time management— it was also rooted in her fear of failure. She would delay starting projects because she was afraid they wouldn't meet her high standards. But by avoiding the work, she was setting herself up for failure. She had become trapped in a cycle of self-doubt and avoidance.

This moment of self-awareness was a breakthrough for Sarah. She understood that acknowledging her weakness didn't mean she was flawed; it meant she had the power to change and improve.

Sarah took actionable steps to address her procrastination. She broke her tasks down into smaller, manageable chunks and set realistic deadlines. She also started to embrace imperfection, understanding that not every project had to be flawless. She learned to prioritise progress over perfection, realising that it was more important to move forward, even with small steps, than to avoid action out of fear.

Through these changes, Sarah's work improved. She found that by tackling her weaknesses head-on, she was able to enhance her strengths even further. No longer burdened by the weight of procrastination, Sarah could dedicate more energy to her creativity and produce her best work without the unnecessary stress.

Strengths and Weaknesses: Two Sides of the Same Coin

Sarah's journey is a reminder that our strengths and weaknesses are often interconnected. Our strengths provide the foundation for success but it's through understanding and working on our weaknesses that we create opportunities for true growth. Here's how you can approach both in your own life:

1. **Recognize Your Strengths:** Begin by identifying your strengths—those qualities that come naturally to you. These are the areas where you excel, whether it's creativity, problem-solving, communication or empathy. Acknowledge them and take pride in them. They are the tools that will help you achieve your goals.

2. **Face Your Weaknesses:** The next step is to identify your weaknesses. This might be harder than recognising your strengths but it's just as important.

   - Are you easily distracted?

   - Do you struggle with confidence?

   - Is perfectionism holding you back?

The key is to approach these weaknesses with compassion, not judgement. Everyone has areas to improve, and acknowledging them is a sign of strength, not weakness.

3. **Develop Strategies for Growth:** Once you've recognised both your strengths and weaknesses, create a plan for growth. Focus on leveraging your strengths to overcome challenges. For example, if you're great at connecting with others but struggle with organisation, use your communication skills to seek support or delegate tasks. When it comes to weaknesses, break them down into manageable steps and set achievable goals. This allows you to make gradual progress without feeling overwhelmed.

4. **Learn to Embrace Imperfection:** Perfectionism often stems from an unwillingness to confront weaknesses. Understand that no one is perfect, and it's okay to have flaws. Instead of viewing weaknesses as failures, see them as areas for improvement and opportunities for growth. Embracing imperfection is liberating—it allows you to move forward without being held back by fear or self-doubt.

5. **Balance Your Strengths and Weaknesses:** The key to personal growth is finding balance. Your strengths are powerful tools but they alone will not make you successful. Likewise, working on your weaknesses is essential but it's equally important to nurture your strengths. Strive to create harmony between the two by using your strengths to support your growth in areas that need improvement.

Understanding your strengths and weaknesses is a transformative act of self-awareness. By embracing both, you empower yourself to take control of your growth journey. You begin to see yourself as a work in progress, constantly evolving, learning and improving.

Remember, you are not defined by your weaknesses nor are you limited by your strengths. You are a combination of both and it's through this balance that you unlock your true potential. By acknowledging your strengths and working on your weaknesses, you take the first step toward becoming the best version of yourself.

In the end, the journey to self-awareness is not about being perfect—it's about understanding who you are, embracing your unique qualities, and using them to live a more authentic, fulfilling life.

4

The Role of Emotions

"You must learn to master your emotions, not suppress them."

Our beliefs shape how we see ourselves but it's our emotions that make these beliefs feel real and impactful. Imagine someone who believes they're not good enough to advance in their career. Each time they consider applying for a new role, a wave of anxiety or self-doubt arises, reinforcing that belief and holding them back. These emotions are powerful—they validate the limiting thoughts and, in doing so, keep us in a cycle of inaction. But what if, instead of letting these emotions dictate our choices, we learned to interpret them as signals for change? By understanding the emotional responses tied to our beliefs, we unlock the possibility of using those same feelings to drive us forward rather than hold us back.

Many of us grow up believing that emotions are something to control or hide, especially in a world that often values logic and toughness over vulnerability. But the truth is, your emotions are powerful messengers, and learning how to understand, embrace and harness them is key to unlocking your full potential.

Emotions are not weaknesses to be suppressed—they are signals. They guide you toward what matters most in your life and indicate areas of growth that demand your attention. Fear, anger, joy, sadness—each emotion carries valuable information. The challenge is learning how to listen and respond to these emotions rather than allowing them to control you or dictate your actions.

Understanding the Emotional Compass

Emotions are your internal compass, pointing you toward the areas of your life where change is needed. For example, feeling stuck in your career might trigger frustration or anxiety. These emotions aren't random—they're telling you something important and that is you're out of alignment with what you truly want.

Rather than ignoring these feelings or numbing them with distractions, ask yourself: What is this emotion trying to tell me? Your emotions are clues to what's happening beneath the surface. By tuning in and reflecting, you can begin to make informed decisions that lead to meaningful change.

The Danger of Emotional Suppression

For years, many of us have been conditioned to "keep it together", to push through tough times without showing vulnerability. But when you suppress emotions, they don't disappear. Instead, they accumulate, becoming mental and physical stressors that eventually explode or manifest in unhealthy ways—whether it's burnout, anxiety, or strained relationships.

Consider this: have you ever held back anger or sadness, only to have it overwhelm you later? Suppression never leads to resolution. Bottling up emotions is like trying to ignore an alarm that's warning you of danger. The more you push them down, the louder they'll return.

Allow yourself to feel fully. This doesn't mean indulging every emotional impulse, but rather, letting yourself experience your emotions without judgement. When you accept them, you can begin to work through them in a healthy way.

Using Emotions as Fuel for Growth

While emotions can sometimes feel like they slow you down, they're also a powerful source of fuel if you use them wisely. Fear, for instance, often paralyses us, but it can also be a catalyst for courage. Think about how many breakthroughs in life have come from moments of fear. Fear tells you that something important is at stake. Instead of letting it stop you, allow it to push you forward. Ask yourself: What's on the other side of this fear?

Similarly, anger, when handled properly, can ignite the fire for change. Many successful people have used the anger they felt about their circumstances as the energy to transform their lives. Anger can inspire action—just as long as it's channelled constructively.

Even emotions like sadness and disappointment have their place. They teach you resilience and patience. When you embrace and work through difficult emotions, you build emotional strength, much like how your muscles grow stronger after resistance training.

Emotional Intelligence: The Game-Changer

Emotional intelligence (EI) is the skill of recognizing, understanding and managing your emotions—and the emotions of others. When you develop emotional intelligence, you gain the ability to stay calm under pressure, manage conflict and build stronger relationships.

Developing emotional intelligence starts with self-awareness. Take time to check in with your emotions throughout the day. Ask yourself how you're feeling and why. Over time, this practice will help you respond rather than react, making you less likely to be swept away by your emotions.

Empathy, another component of EI, allows you to connect deeply with others. The more you understand your own emotions, the better equipped you are to understand those of others. This ability can enhance both personal and professional relationships, creating stronger connections that support your growth.

Transforming Your Emotional Mindset

Ultimately, emotions are part of what makes you human—and powerful. Conquering the battle within you, emotions are not the enemy. They are tools. Learning how to recognise, process and harness your emotions will transform the way you experience life and approach your challenges.

To begin transforming your emotional mindset:

- **Acknowledge your emotions:** When they arise, don't push them away. Understand them and give yourself permission to feel them.

- **Ask what they're teaching you:** Every emotion carries a message. Find out what your emotions are telling you about your desires, fears or areas of growth.

- **Channel them productively:** Use your emotions as fuel. Let fear drive you toward courage. Let frustration motivate you to create change. Let joy remind you of what's most important.

Lucky, my classmate, was a backbencher since childhood. We always heard that teachers and others used to throw insults and negative words towards him. The constant comparison with his peers during childhood didn't feel much but at a young age he feels angry. He always listens to the similar words: "You're worthless, you'll never succeed."

The fear of failure leads to the feelings of anger and frustration. He started feeling self-doubt and anxiety.

Lucky retreats into social media or procrastination, venting his frustration online instead of confronting the root of his feelings.

Instead of transforming his anger into constructive action, Lucky gets caught in a cycle of frustration and dissatisfaction, which can lead to feelings of hopelessness and burnout. He becomes desensitised to the issues he cares about, and his anger ultimately turns inward, leading to feelings of futility rather than motivating him to make a difference.

One day, the words "You'll never succeed" hit him hard, echoing in his mind long after they were spoken. Initially, he felt a wave of anger and frustration wash over him; those words felt like a weight pressing down on his aspirations. But as he sat in his room that evening, reflecting on the situation, something shifted within him. Instead of allowing those words to define his future, he decided to use them as fuel for change.

Lucky began to transform his anger into determination. He thought about what success meant to him and how much he wanted to prove not only to others but also to himself that he was capable of achieving his goals. He started by setting clear, achievable objectives. Rather than feeling overwhelmed by the thought of failure, he focused on small, manageable steps that could lead him to success.

Lucky strived to turn his initial frustration into a proactive approach to learning. Every time he encountered a challenge, he reminded himself of the people's words, using that anger as motivation to push harder.

As weeks turned into months, Lucky began to see significant progress. His confidence grew. He participated more actively. The anger that once felt like a burden became a driving force, igniting a passion for learning and a desire to succeed.

He realised that the words spoken to him didn't have to dictate his path; rather, they became a turning point that propelled him forward. His journey taught him that success is not defined by the doubts of others but by one's determination to rise above challenges and strive for greatness.

This experience transformed Lucky, not just academically but also personally. He learned that anger, when harnessed positively, could serve as a powerful catalyst for change, motivating him to pursue his dreams with vigour and confidence. Ultimately, Lucky's story is a testament to the idea that our responses to setbacks shape our futures, and that success often emerges from the ashes of frustration and doubt. Today, he stands as a successful businessman.

In the end, mastering your emotions is about self-mastery. It's about learning to work with yourself rather than against yourself. Emotions are the bridge between who you are and who you are becoming. Let them guide you, fuel you, and most importantly, help you grow.

Remember: The key to personal growth isn't in avoiding emotions but embracing them as your greatest teachers.

"Emotions, the colours that paint our soul,
They guide our steps, they make us whole.
A compass through the highs and lows,
In every tear and joy, we grow."

5

Defining Core Values and Purpose

"Purpose is the foundation; core values are the pillars that support a life of meaning and fulfilment."

In our fast-paced world, it's easy to lose sight of what truly matters. We can get caught up in daily tasks, social expectations and the pursuit of success without stopping to ask ourselves:

- What is my purpose?

- What values guide my life?

But these questions are essential for creating a meaningful, fulfilling life. Your core values and purpose are the foundation upon which you can build a life of intention— one that aligns with your true self and sets a clear direction for your decisions and long-term goals.

The Power of Core Values and Purpose

Core values are the guiding principles that define what you stand for and influence how you act, even when nobody's watching. They represent what you believe in most deeply like honesty, compassion or courage. Purpose, on the other hand, is your "why"—the reason behind your actions and aspirations. When you have a clear purpose, your life has direction and meaning.

Together, your core values and purpose act as a compass, steering you toward a life that feels true to you, regardless of circumstances. They help you make decisions with clarity, prioritise what really matters and set goals that resonate with your deepest aspirations. In short, they form the foundation for a life of meaning, integrity and fulfilment.

Why Core Values and Purpose Matter?

Without core values and purpose, it's easy to feel lost, constantly chasing after things that don't truly satisfy you. Defining these inner principles not only provides stability in challenging times but also enables you to move confidently toward a future that aligns with who you are. With core values and purpose in place, every choice you make becomes more meaningful, intentional and fulfilling.

Let me now take you to Mayra's journey to purpose.

Mayra had always been ambitious. From a young age, she excelled academically and pursued a high-powered career in finance. But after years of climbing the corporate ladder, Mayra began to feel an emptiness that success alone couldn't fill. She was financially secure, respected in her field and admired by others, yet something crucial was missing.

One day, Mayra was volunteering at a community shelter. She noticed how much she enjoyed helping others find stability in their lives, listening to their struggles and offering support. She felt a sense of fulfilment she hadn't felt in years. For the first time, she realised that compassion and service to others were her true values—not just ambition or financial success.

Mayra decided to take a bold step. She redefined her career path to include meaningful work that aligned with her core values. Over time, she transitioned from finance to nonprofit work, where she felt she could make a more significant difference. Today, Mayra feels fulfilled because her work aligns with her values of compassion, empathy and purpose. She no longer measures success by financial gain alone but by the positive impact she can make.

Defining Your Core Values

Your core values are unique to you. Here's how you can identify them:

1. **Reflect on Past Experiences:** Think back to times when you felt proud, fulfilled, or disappointed. What was it about those moments that made you feel that way? Often, these experiences highlight your core values. For instance, if you felt fulfilled when standing up for someone, fairness or courage might be a core value.

2. **Identify Key Qualities:** Make a list of qualities that you respect and admire in yourself and others. These might include integrity, kindness, resilience or creativity. Narrow the list down to your top five to seven values—the ones that resonate most deeply with who you are.

3. **Consider What Brings You Joy:** Think about activities or relationships that bring you joy and satisfaction. Are there common themes in these moments? For example, if teaching others or learning new things brings you joy then knowledge or growth may be core values.

Discovering Your Purpose

Purpose is often found at the intersection of your passions, strengths and values. It's your reason for being—the unique contribution you want to make to the world. Here's a process for discovering it:

1. **Identify Your Passions and Strengths:** Ask yourself:

   - What activities make me lose track of time?

   - What am I naturally good at?

   These clues can reveal your passions and strengths which are often tied to your purpose.

2. **Ask "Why" Questions:** Reflect on why certain activities matter to you. For example, if you love helping others, ask yourself why. You may find that you want to create a world where people feel supported and understood.

3. **Write a Personal Mission Statement:** Using your values, passions and strengths, write a mission statement that captures your purpose. It doesn't have to be perfect; the goal is to summarise what you hope to achieve and contribute to the world. For example, my purpose is to inspire others to reach their full potential through empathy, guidance and support.

4. **Live Your Purpose in Small Ways:** Start incorporating your purpose into your daily life. Purpose isn't just about grand actions; it's about living intentionally every day. If your purpose is to uplift others, find small ways to do that, like offering encouragement or sharing knowledge.

Making Values-Based Decisions

Once you've defined your core values and purpose, use them to guide your decisions. Before making a choice, ask yourself:

- Does this align with my core values?

- Will this bring me closer to fulfilling my purpose?

- Does this choice reflect who I want to be and what I want to achieve?

When decisions align with your values and purpose, they become easier to make, and you feel more confident in your choices. This approach not only keeps you on track but also brings you a sense of peace, knowing that you're living in alignment with who you truly are.

Embracing Core Values in Decision-Making

Consider Priya, a corporate lawyer who values integrity, compassion and justice. She's passionate about making a difference and had always wanted to pursue a career in public interest law. However, the financial security of her current job made it hard for her to leave.

After defining her core values and purpose, Priya realised that her current job was in direct conflict with her values. She felt increasingly unfulfilled, knowing she wasn't living her purpose. With her values as her compass, Priya made the tough decision to transition into public interest law, even though it meant a financial adjustment. Today, she works for a nonprofit organisation that aligns with her values of justice and compassion, and she feels a greater sense of fulfilment and purpose.

Living a Meaningful Life

Defining and living by your core values and purpose transforms your life. It helps you set meaningful goals and make decisions with confidence, knowing they align with your deeper principles. Rather than chasing fleeting achievements, you create a life that is deeply rewarding and true to who you are.

A meaningful life isn't about accumulating accomplishments—it's about living with intention. When your actions reflect your core values and purpose, you leave a legacy that goes beyond material success. You inspire others, uplift those around you and contribute to a world where people are empowered to live authentically.

Crafting Your Compass for Life

It's a lifelong journey of self-awareness, refinement and intentionality. You may face challenges and obstacles, but with your values and purpose as your guide, you can navigate through uncertainty with confidence. You'll know that every decision, no matter how big or small, is part of a greater picture—a life lived with meaning, purpose and integrity.

As you continue on this journey, remember that living a purposeful and values-based life is the greatest gift you can give yourself and the world. It's the path to genuine fulfilment and the key to building a life that truly matters.

6

Developing Growth Mindset

"Your mindset is the key to unlocking your potential."

At the heart of personal transformation lies a powerful concept: mindset. The way we perceive ourselves, our abilities and the world around us, shapes our experiences and outcomes. This chapter explores the critical transition from a fixed mindset to a growth mindset—a shift that can unlock untapped potential and lead to profound personal growth.

Mindsets are the beliefs we hold about our abilities and intelligence. According to psychologist Carol Dweck, there are two primary types of mindsets: fixed and growth. A fixed mindset believes that our abilities are static and unchangeable. People with this mindset often avoid challenges, give up easily, and see efforts as fruitless. In contrast, a growth mindset embraces challenges, sees failures as opportunities for learning and values effort as a pathway to mastery.

Anjali, an UPSC aspirant, struggles with different subjects and language barriers. With a fixed mindset, Anjali might believe that "she is not enough". This belief leads her to shy away from challenging courses and ultimately reinforces her self-doubt. However, if Anjali were to cultivate a growth mindset, she would recognise that with practice and perseverance, she could improve skills.

Living with a fixed mindset can severely limit potential. When we view our abilities as fixed traits, we tend to shy away from risk and challenges. This avoidance creates a cycle of stagnation where we miss opportunities for growth and learning.

The Power of Growth Mindset

Shifting to a growth mindset can be transformative. By embracing the belief that abilities can be developed through dedication and hard work, we open ourselves up to a world of possibilities. This mindset encourages resilience, curiosity and a passion for learning.

Priyanka, a young entrepreneur, exemplifies this shift. After facing multiple failures in her business ventures, she initially felt defeated and considered giving up. However, upon reflecting on her experiences, she realised that each setback provided valuable lessons. By adopting a growth mindset, Priyanka began to view challenges as stepping stones rather than obstacles. She sought feedback, adjusted her strategies and eventually found success in her endeavours.

The Role of Self-Talk

Self-talk plays a significant role in shaping our mindset. The language we use with ourselves can reinforce a fixed or growth mindset. Pay attention to your internal dialogues— are you focusing on limitations or possibilities?

Aditi, a college student, often found herself saying, "I can't do this. I'm not smart enough." This self-talk reinforced her fixed mindset, leading her to avoid challenging courses. However, after recognising the negative impact of these thoughts, he began to replace them with affirmations like, "I may struggle now but I can learn and improve with effort." This simple shift transformed his approach to learning.

FIXED MINDSET	GROWTH MINDSET
I am not talented enough to succeed.	I will learn and put effort into succeeding.
I quit.	Making mistakes and learning from it to get better.
I hate new challenges because I just can't do it.	I love new challenges.
I am who I am.	I can become the person I want to be.
Threatened by others' success.	Inspired by others' success.
Others are correct, I am not good enough.	Others do not dictate my success and I embrace criticism.

Overcoming Obstacles to Change

While the benefits of a growth mindset are clear, the journey to cultivate it can be challenging. Old habits and deeply ingrained beliefs can resist change. It's essential to approach this process with patience and self-compassion, by treating yourself with kindness during moments of failure and gradually you'll rewire your thinking and embrace the growth mindset.

The mindset shift from fixed to growth is not the destination but a continuous journey. It requires ongoing reflections, practice and a commitment to self-improvement.

By accepting challenges, reframing failure and fostering a positive internal dialogues, we can cultivate a growth mindset that empowers us to reach our fullest potential.

As you embark on your journey of self-discovery, remember that you have the power to shape your mindset. Each challenge you face is an opportunity for growth and every failure is a stepping stone to success. The battle of "You vs You" is a testament to your resilience and capacity for change.

Embrace the mindset shift and unlock the limitless possibilities that await you. The journey is yours and the growth is boundless.

"Whether you think you can, or you think you can't,
you're right."

~ **Henry Ford**

PART TWO

Self-Discipline

7

Setting Clear Goals

Setting Effective Goals

There are three steps that shall help you to set clear and effective goals:

- Transforms ambition into achievement

- Provide direction and purpose in your journey

- Define goals clearly, and let them guide your actions

Setting effective goals is a powerful practice that can transform your aspirations into tangible achievements. However, the process goes beyond mere planning; it involves self-discovery, motivation and a clear vision for your future. This chapter provides a practical blueprint for setting and achieving goals that align with your purpose, ensuring that you live your life fully and authentically.

The Importance of Effective Goal Setting

Effective goal setting serves as a roadmap for your life. It helps you focus your energy, prioritise your time and measure your progress. When your goals are well-defined, they become a source of motivation that propels you forward even in the face of obstacles.

Step 1: Set SMART Goals

Once you've clarified your values, it's time to set SMART goals—Specific, Measurable, Achievable, Relevant and Time-bound. This framework ensures your goals are clear and attainable. Here's how to apply each element:

- **Specific:** Clearly define what you want to achieve.

- **Measurable:** Establish criteria to track your progress.

- **Achievable:** Set goals that are realistic and attainable. Consider your current circumstances and resources.

- **Relevant:** Ensure your goals align with your core values and purpose.

- **Time-bound:** Set a deadline for achieving your goals. This creates urgency and helps you stay focused.

Step 2: Break Goals into Actionable Steps

Setting a big goal can be overwhelming but breaking it down into smaller, manageable steps makes it more achievable.

Step 3: Stay Committed and Adapt

Commitment is crucial in achieving your goals. However, life is unpredictable and circumstances may change. Here are strategies to maintain commitment while allowing for adaptability:

- **Be Flexible:** If you encounter obstacles or your priorities change, be willing to adjust your goals. Flexibility allows you to respond to life's challenges without losing sight of your overall vision.

- **Monitor and reflect regularly:** Set aside time to review your progress. Ask yourself:

  - What's working?

  - What isn't?

  - What can I change?

Reflecting helps you stay on track and adapt to challenges effectively.

Reframe Challenges as Opportunities

View obstacles as chances to grow and learn rather than reasons to quit.

Develop a problem-solving mindset to tackle issues creatively and keep moving forward.

- **Stay Grounded in Your Purpose:** Remind yourself of why you started this journey. Reconnect with the deeper meaning behind your goals to maintain motivation during tough times.

Step 4: Reflect and Celebrate

Reflection is a vital part of the goal-setting process. Regularly take time to assess your progress.

Setting effective goals is an empowering practice that can lead to a more fulfilling life and you can navigate the journey of life with intention and clarity.

Remember, you only live once. Embrace this journey and set goals that inspire you to overcome obstacles, fulfil your wishes, and live authentically. With each goal achieved, you'll not only be one step closer to your dreams but also cultivate a deeper understanding of yourself and your purpose. The journey is yours—make it extraordinary.

"Shape your vision, set it high,
Step by step, you'll touch the sky.
With focus sharp and will aligned,
Your goals will meet the strength of mind."

8

Building Habits

"The quality of your habits determines the quality of your life."

In life, the road to success is often built on small, consistent actions rather than grand, sudden achievements. This is the power of habits—they are the quiet, daily steps that drive real, lasting change. But building sustainable habits isn't just about motivation. It's about crafting routines that feel natural and essential, something you do without even thinking.

Meet Arjun, a 40-year-old father and a project manager with a hectic schedule. For years, Arjun dreamed of getting into shape and eating healthier, but his demanding job and family obligations left little time or energy for big lifestyle changes. He had tried making drastic shifts—signing up for intense workout programs and restrictive diets—but they never lasted beyond a few weeks. Frustrated, he decided to try a different approach.

Instead of jumping into an intense routine, Arjun began with a small habit: he committed to doing just five push-ups every morning, no matter how busy he was. Five push-ups took him less than a minute, making it hard to skip. This small action felt achievable and didn't disrupt his schedule. Arjun kept up with this habit for a month, finding that the quick burst of energy started his day on a positive note.

As weeks went by, Arjun naturally began to crave a bit more movement in the mornings. He added five squats to his routine and then a few more stretches. Over a few months, his five push-ups had evolved into a 15-minute morning workout. Encouraged by his progress, he began making healthier breakfast choices, adding a fruit or smoothie to start his day.

This entire transformation started from a habit so simple it felt effortless. Arjun didn't rely on motivation or willpower to overhaul his lifestyle. By beginning with something small and doable, he built momentum and confidence, which fueled his next steps.

Why Tiny Habits Work?

Arjun's success stemmed from a few key principles of habit-building:

1. Start Small

Effective habits are those that feel manageable. Arjun's initial commitment to just five push-ups made his goal easy to stick with, reducing the likelihood of giving up. Starting small builds consistency without overwhelming you.

2. Focus on Repetition, Not Intensity

Arjun's priority was consistency, not creating a full workout routine. Repetition is what strengthens neural pathways, making the behaviour automatic over time. A habit doesn't need to be intense—it just needs to be regular.

3. Stack New Habits on Existing Ones

Once he was consistently doing push-ups, Arjun added another action—five squats. Building on an existing habit, known as habit stacking, helps create a sequence that feels natural and sustainable.

Practical Steps to Build Lasting Habits

- **Choose a Keystone Habit**

A keystone habit is a small, manageable action that can inspire positive change in other areas of your life. Arjun's five push-ups each morning were his keystone habit, a foundation that led to more changes in his routine.

- **Keep It Easy**

When starting a habit, think small. Want to meditate? Begin with one deep breath every morning. Want to eat healthier? Start by adding a piece of fruit to one meal. These tiny habits build consistency without requiring extreme effort.

- **Set Reminders and Cues**

Link your new habit to an existing part of your day. Arjun's cue was waking up. By connecting habits to daily routines, you can make them feel like a natural part of your day.

- **Track Your Progress**

Tracking doesn't have to be complicated; a simple mark on a calendar each day you complete your habit can reinforce your progress and help you stay accountable.

- **Embrace Imperfection**

Missing a day doesn't mean your habit is broken. Habits take time to solidify, and setbacks are normal. What matters is getting back on track and focusing on long-term consistency.

Why Small Habits Lead to Big Changes?

The true power of habits lies in their cumulative effect. Small actions, when done consistently, can create profound results. Arjun's journey to better health wasn't a sudden transformation but a series of small, sustainable steps.

Building habits isn't about willpower or dramatic changes—it's about creating a life that works for you, one small step at a time. Start small, stay consistent and let each habit become a stepping stone toward lasting change.

The path to transformation isn't about reaching the finish line immediately; it's about committing to simple, meaningful steps that, repeated over time, create the life you envision.

9

Mastering Time Management

"Time is the one resource you can't get back– use it wisely."

Time is a resource we all share, yet how we use it determines much of our success and satisfaction. Mastering time management isn't about cramming more into each day, but about making intentional choices that maximise productivity and minimise distractions.

1. Set Clear Priorities

Identify what matters most. Clear priorities help you know where to invest your energy. Ask yourself: Which tasks will bring me closer to my goals? Focus on high-impact activities that yield meaningful results.

Example: Successful people often dedicate their mornings to their most important work, like strategising or creating, before tackling less critical tasks. This ensures that the majority of their day is spent productively.

2. Use the Four Quadrant Technique

One of the most effective tools for prioritising tasks is the Four Quadrant Technique, also known as the Eisenhower Matrix. This method helps categorise tasks based on urgency and importance, allowing you to make smarter time management choices.

Quadrant 1: Urgent and Important

Tasks that require immediate attention, such as deadlines and crises. Handle these first.

Quadrant 2: Important but Not Urgent

Tasks that lead to long-term success, like planning, strategizing, and self-care. Prioritise these to prevent them from becoming urgent.

Quadrant 3: Urgent but Not Important

Tasks that need attention but don't contribute significantly to your goals, like some emails and meetings. Delegate or limit time spent here.

Quadrant 4: Not Urgent and Not Important

Low-value tasks, often distractions, such as excessive social media. Eliminate or minimise these.

3. Use Time Blocks

Time blocking means scheduling dedicated periods for specific tasks. Instead of multitasking, you focus on one task at a time within set blocks, promoting deep, uninterrupted work.

4. Limit Distractions

In a world full of digital noise, reducing distractions is crucial. Silence notifications, close unnecessary tabs and set boundaries to protect your focus.

5. Learn to Say No

Effective time management also means setting boundaries. Saying "no" to tasks that don't align with your goals allows you to protect your time for what truly matters.

6. Reflect and Adjust

Reflect on what worked, what didn't and where you can improve. Time management is a skill that develops with practice and reflection.

10

Kicking Out Distractions

In a world where distractions are only a swipe or click away, staying focused has become a skill. Distractions dilute our productivity and prevent us from reaching our potential.

- **Identify Your Distractions**

The first step to managing distractions is awareness. Ask yourself: What usually pulls me away from my tasks? Common distractions might include social media, notifications or even internal thoughts.

- **Control Your Digital Environment**

Digital distractions are the most persistent. Set up your devices for productivity by silencing notifications and logging out of non-essential apps during focused work.

- **The Power of Deep Work**

Deep work involves uninterrupted, focused time on a single task. Schedule specific blocks each day for this. During deep work, eliminate as many distractions as possible and focus solely on the task at hand.

Use a timer, like the Pomodoro Technique—25 minutes of work, followed by a 5-minute break—to stay concentrated.

- **Set Boundaries**

Boundaries signal to yourself and others that you're in focus mode. If you're working from home, let family or roommates know when you need uninterrupted time.

Example: Blocking off certain hours as "focus hours" can also reduce interruptions and help you get into a flow state.

- **Redirect Internal Distractions**

Sometimes, distractions come from within—thoughts, worries or urges to procrastinate. Acknowledge these thoughts, then gently guide your mind back to the task. Practising mindfulness or using short breathing exercises can improve focus and reduce stress.

- **Take Regular Breaks**

Ironically, focusing too long without a break can lead to mental fatigue and make distractions harder to resist. Regular, intentional breaks improve your ability to focus when you return.

Overcoming distractions requires discipline, strategy and practice. By mastering these skills, you'll reclaim control of your time, improve your productivity and take charge of your path toward success.

Six ways to be super productive:

1. Prioritise task
2. Set clear goals
3. Time manage
4. Minimise distractions
5. Break and rest
6. Continuous learn

11

The Power of Routine and Consistency

"Success is built in steps so small,
Each day we rise, each day we fall.
Through quiet acts, we shape our way,
And greatness grows with each new day."

Consistency is the unseen thread that weaves the fabric of success. In a world where instant gratification has become the norm, the real power lies in what we do repeatedly, not occasionally. The ability to show up, day after day, regardless of how we feel, is the secret behind all lasting achievement. This is the essence of The Consistency Code—a formula not built on sporadic bursts of effort, but on the quiet, relentless power of routine.

The Silent Force of Habits

Habits are the building blocks of our lives yet their power is often underestimated. What we do consistently, we eventually become. Routine is like the steady pulse that keeps life moving forward, often unnoticed yet vital to our progress. Think of a river—its flow is soft, but over time it carves through mountains. This is the power of routine in action. The small, everyday choices accumulate to create monumental change, even though we don't see the results overnight.

But the magic of routine is not only in its results; it's in the process. By establishing a routine, we take the guesswork out of life. The discipline of doing something daily frees us from the trap of relying on motivation. Motivation is fleeting—it comes and goes with our moods—but routine, once established, becomes second nature. It anchors us when our emotions would otherwise throw us off course.

The Myth of Motivation

We've all been sold the myth that motivation is the driving force behind achievement. We wait for the right mood, the perfect inspiration or the energy to start something new. But the truth is—motivation is unreliable. It's like a spark; it can ignite something within you but it's the slow, steady burn of consistency that keeps the fire alive. Routine, not motivation, is what drives long-term success.

Those who rely solely on motivation will find themselves in an endless cycle of peaks and valleys—great bursts of energy followed by periods of stagnation. But those who follow the Consistency Code understand that progress is made not in the moments of inspiration, but in the quiet, often unremarkable days of showing up, again and again, regardless of how they feel.

Designing Your Daily Rhythm

Building a powerful routine doesn't happen by accident—it's intentional. It starts with small, manageable actions that can be repeated day after day. Success isn't found in grand gestures but in the simplicity of doing the right things consistently.

To create your own Consistency Code, ask yourself: What are the core actions that will lead me to my goals? Identify them and then make them non-negotiable. This could be as simple as committing to a daily workout, setting aside time for learning or dedicating an hour each day to a passion project. The key is to make these actions a priority and to integrate them into your daily life in a way that feels sustainable.

The hardest part of creating a routine is starting small. We often overestimate what we can achieve in the short term and underestimate the power of small, consistent efforts over time. Instead of trying to overhaul your entire life in one go, start with one or two habits. Master them, make them part of your daily rhythm and then gradually add more.

Mastering the Mundane

Routine is not glamorous. There's no excitement in waking up at the same time every day, practising the same skills or following a repetitive schedule. But therein lies its beauty. Mastering the mundane is what separates the dreamers from the achievers. The most successful people in the world didn't get there by accident—they built their success through a series of unremarkable, consistent actions over time.

Think of athletes who train every single day, writers who write even when inspiration is nowhere to be found or entrepreneurs who work on their businesses relentlessly. They have mastered the art of doing the same things over and over again, knowing that excellence is a result of repetition, not bursts of effort.

When you embrace routine, you become immune to the

distractions that derail others. You don't need to wait for the perfect time to start—you just do it. You don't need permission from motivation to act—you simply follow the path you've set for yourself. This is the power of consistency.

Breaking Through Resistance

Resistance is inevitable. There will be days when everything in you screams to quit, when the routine feels like a burden rather than a blessing. But the Consistency Code teaches us that these moments are where growth happens. It's in the moments of resistance, when you want to give up, that the real transformation occurs.

Consistency builds resilience. It teaches you to push through discomfort, to persevere even when the results aren't immediately visible. Over time, this persistence not only brings success but also strengthens your character. You become someone who can be relied upon, not just by others but by yourself. You begin to trust in your ability to follow through, no matter what.

The Compound Effect

The true power of routine lies in what's known as the compound effect. Small, consistent actions, when done over time, produce exponential results. Think of how saving a small amount of money every day, over the course of years, builds wealth. The same principle applies to every area of life—whether it's fitness, learning or personal development. Each small action compounds, growing in power until the results are undeniable.

This is why routine is so transformative. It doesn't rely on huge leaps forward. Instead, it focuses on steady, consistent progress. And over time, this progress builds momentum, leading to breakthroughs that feel almost effortless.

The Consistency Code is not about perfection. It's about persistence. It's about trusting in the power of small actions and showing up for yourself day after day, even when it's hard. The power of routine lies in its ability to create lasting change, one small step at a time.

When you unlock the Consistency Code, you unlock the secret to sustainable success. It's not glamorous but it's powerful.

"Commitment to routine is the bridge between intention and achievement."

12

Self-Accountability and Progress Tracking

Self-accountability is the cornerstone that keeps you grounded and moving forward. Without it, dreams remain just that—dreams, unattainable and distant. Self-accountability is not about punishing yourself for your mistakes, but rather taking full responsibility for your actions, choices, and the path you take toward your aspirations. It's about creating a system of commitment that drives you, and learning from every step, whether you stumble or soar.

Understanding Self-Accountability

Self-accountability is the ability to hold yourself responsible for your actions and their outcomes. Unlike external accountability, where you rely on others to ensure you stay on track, self-accountability comes from within. It's about taking ownership of your journey—no matter the circumstances, you are the one who decides your response, your next steps, and how you progress.

When you are accountable to yourself, you begin to develop the discipline and resilience needed to succeed.

You take the power to shape your life, knowing that the decisions you make today will affect the outcome of tomorrow. It is no longer about waiting for motivation to hit you; instead, you become the driving force of your own life.

Why Self-Accountability Matters

- **Clarity and Purpose:** When you are accountable to yourself, you clarify your goals and understand why they matter. You no longer drift aimlessly but act with a sense of purpose.

- **Consistency:** Self-accountability pushes you to stay consistent, even when it gets tough. It helps you break through inertia and avoid procrastination.

- **Growth Mindset:** Being accountable means you're not afraid to face your shortcomings. When you take responsibility for where you are, you are more willing to learn, adapt and grow.

- **Improved Decision Making:** Accountability forces you to be mindful of the choices you make, leading to better decision-making skills in all areas of life.

The Role of Tracking Your Progress

Tracking progress is one of the most effective ways to stay accountable. It turns your goals into tangible steps and helps you visualise your progress. Without tracking, it's easy to lose sight of how far you've come and get discouraged by how far you have left to go.

Overcoming the Hurdles of Self-Accountability

While self-accountability is essential, it's not always easy. There will be moments of doubt, times when progress feels slow or situations where you feel like giving up. These are the moments where self-accountability truly comes into play. Here's how to overcome common hurdles:

- **Avoiding Perfectionism:** Perfectionism can be a roadblock to progress. Remember that progress doesn't always look clean or linear. There will be setbacks, but the key is to keep moving forward.

- **Avoiding the Blame Game:** It's easy to blame external factors or circumstances but true self-accountability means taking responsibility, even for things outside your control. Own your choices and your reaction to life's challenges.

- **Staying Motivated:** Motivation wanes but discipline doesn't. Keep tracking your progress even when it feels monotonous. Remind yourself why you started in the first place.

When you track your progress and hold yourself accountable, you are no longer waiting for external validation. You validate yourself. This intrinsic motivation becomes the foundation of your success, and every achievement, no matter how small, becomes a testament to your growth.

Self-accountability isn't just a habit; it's a mindset shift that leads to lasting change. By taking ownership of your actions, tracking your progress and staying committed to your goals, you unlock a powerful force within you. No one else can define your success; it's entirely up to you.

PART THREE
Mental and Physical Well-being

13

Prioritising Self-Care

"You can't pour from an empty cup.
Take care of yourself first."

In a world that never stops moving, it's easy to forget one of the most fundamental aspects of living a balanced, fulfilling life—self-care. We often juggle work, relationships, responsibilities and personal goals, leaving little room for ourselves. But here's the truth: you can't pour from an empty cup. If you want to show up as your best self in all areas of your life, you need to take care of yourself first. Prioritising self-care is not just a luxury; it's a necessity.

Self-care isn't about indulgence or pampering yourself on rare occasions—it's about creating a sustainable, holistic practice that nurtures your physical, mental and emotional well-being every day. It's about making intentional choices that restore your energy, revitalise your spirit and help you navigate life with resilience.

The Foundation of Self-Care

Many people view self-care as a one-time activity—a bubble bath, a weekend getaway or a treat after a long week. While these moments are valuable, self-care is about far more than temporary relief. It's about consistently tending to your needs so that you can maintain balance and health in all aspects of your life.

When you prioritise self-care, you're improving your physical health, boosting your mental clarity and enhancing your emotional resilience. By setting aside time for yourself, you become better equipped to handle stress, make clear decisions and maintain healthy relationships.

Physical Self-Care: Nourishing Your Body

Our bodies are the vessels that carry us through life so it only makes sense to treat them with care. Physical self-care includes the basics: exercise, proper nutrition, hydration and sleep. But it also goes beyond these to include things like taking breaks during long hours of work.

Exercise is particularly vital because it boosts energy levels, reduces stress and promotes better mental health. Whether it's a walk in the park, a yoga session or an intense workout, moving your body is essential for both your physical and mental well-being.

Sleep is another cornerstone of self-care. Inadequate rest affects mood, cognitive function and overall health. Prioritising quality sleep means creating a peaceful nighttime routine, avoiding excessive screen time before bed and ensuring your sleeping environment promotes relaxation.

Mental Self-Care: Sharpening Your Mind

Just as you nurture your body, your mind needs attention and care. Mental self-care focuses on activities that reduce stress, boost focus and keep your mind sharp. This includes practices such as mindfulness, meditation, journaling and engaging in hobbies that promote relaxation and creativity.

One of the most effective ways to nurture your mental health is by practising mindfulness—the art of being fully present in the moment. This helps you reduce anxiety, combat negative thinking and increase overall mental clarity. Whether through guided meditation or simply focusing on your breath for a few minutes each day, mindfulness can help you slow down and manage the overwhelming demands of life.

Incorporate mindfulness into your daily routine even if it's just for 5 minutes. Sit quietly, close your eyes and focus on your breathing. Allow yourself to fully embrace the present moment without distractions.

Emotional Self-Care: Protecting Your Inner Peace

Emotional self-care is all about cultivating a healthy emotional life. This involves managing your emotions, setting boundaries, expressing your feelings and making time for activities that make you feel happy and fulfilled. It's about being kind to yourself and allowing space for rest and reflection when needed.

Many people neglect their emotional health by suppressing feelings or ignoring emotional needs. But your emotions are signals that need to be acknowledged, not ignored. Practising emotional self-care could involve journaling to process your feelings, talking to a trusted friend or therapist or simply giving yourself permission to rest without guilt.

Setting healthy boundaries is a key aspect of emotional self-care. Saying no when something doesn't align with your needs or values is not selfish; it's an act of self-respect. Protecting your energy from toxic people or situations ensures that you can nurture your inner peace.

Social Self-Care: Cultivating Meaningful Connections

Humans are social creatures, and social self-care involves creating and maintaining positive, supportive relationships. Strong social connections can improve your mood, provide a sense of belonging, and offer a support network during tough times. But social self-care isn't just about being surrounded by others—it's about cultivating meaningful interactions that nourish you.

Spending time with friends, family or a supportive community can help combat loneliness and increase your overall happiness. But it's also important to create time for yourself even if it means saying no to social invitations when you need rest.

Spiritual Self-Care: Nurturing Your Inner Spirit

Spirituality doesn't necessarily mean religion—it can also refer to your connection to something larger than yourself, your sense of purpose or your inner peace. Spiritual self-care is about finding practices that help you feel grounded, aligned, and at peace with yourself and the world around you.

For some, this might involve prayer or meditation, while for others it could mean spending time in nature, practising gratitude or reflecting on personal values and goals. Nurturing your spiritual self is about connecting with your deeper sense of meaning and purpose.

Self-Compassion: Being Your Own Best Friend

Perhaps the most important aspect of self-care is self-compassion. This means treating yourself with the same kindness, concern, and understanding that you would offer a friend. It's about accepting your imperfections and showing yourself love, even when you make mistakes.

Often, we are our own harshest critics, but self-compassion is the key to maintaining mental and emotional health. When you're kind to yourself, you reduce stress, boost self-esteem and foster a positive, resilient mindset.

A healthy mind and body start with the simple decision to put yourself first. You're your greatest asset—prioritise self-care to keep growing and thriving.

14

Overcoming Overthinking

"Overthinking is a misuse of your imagination—focus on what you can control and create clarity."

Imagine it's 2 a.m. and you're lying in bed, desperately wanting to fall asleep. But your mind feels like a movie reel, playing out scene after scene of past conversations, unfinished tasks, worries about tomorrow and random "what if" scenarios. It's quiet outside yet in your mind, it's as if there's a crowd all talking at once. You replay moments, wonder if you made the right choices and start doubting yourself.

Maybe you think about a comment someone made during the day and wonder what they really meant. Or you worry about an upcoming meeting, rehearsing what you'll say, as if the "perfect" words will make everything go smoothly. Thoughts jump from one worry to another, and you lie there, wide awake, exhausted but unable to silence your mind. This cycle keeps you trapped in an exhausting mental loop that drains your energy, makes you more anxious and keeps you from the rest you need.

Kavya, a 25-year-old content creator, spent hours on social media every day, comparing herself to others. Her feed was filled with influencers and peers who seemed to have it all—perfect careers, relationships, and lifestyles.

Why can't I be as successful as them? she thought, scrolling through their posts. I've been trying so hard, but my content doesn't get the attention theirs does. Maybe I'm just not good enough. She began to replay moments from her past—how she had struggled to find her voice as a creator, and how some of her early videos hadn't gained much traction.

What if I never make it? What if this is as far as I go? Her mind shifted to the future, filled with worries. *What if I fall behind? What if I keep failing and lose my audience?*

The pressure to keep up with others grew unbearable and the fear of not measuring up consumed her.

Kavya's overthinking paralyzed her. Instead of creating new content, she spent hours obsessing over old posts, analysing every like, comment, and view. She felt like she was always falling short, trapped between regret over past mistakes and anxiety about future failures.

One day, a friend noticed her frustration and said, "Kavya, you can't keep comparing yourself to everyone else. You're living in the shadow of your past mistakes and the uncertainty of your future. What you can control is today—just create for the joy of it, not for validation. Guilt cannot change the past; it only burdens the present. No amount of anxiety can build a better tomorrow; only actions can."

Her friend's words hit home. Kavya realised that her constant overthinking about the past and future had stopped her from doing what she loved—creating content. She decided to let go of comparisons, focusing instead on her own growth and progress.

Kavya began posting with confidence, not worrying about the number of views or likes. She stopped trying to live up to others' standards and started embracing her own journey. Over time, her audience grew—not because she was perfect, but because she was authentic.

Overthinking, especially fueled by social media, keeps you stuck in the past and paralyses you about the future. The key to overcoming it is focusing on the present moment and creating for yourself, not for approval.

"Free your mind from endless thoughts; clarity begins where overthinking ends."

Breaking the Cycle of Overthinking

Overcoming overthinking is about reclaiming control of your mind and shifting from rumination to purposeful action. Instead of fixating on "what if" scenarios, shift your focus to "how can I solve this?"

Let's say you're worried about a project deadline. Instead of spinning in anxiety, ask, "What's the first step I can take?"

Solutions-oriented thinking frees you from circular worry and puts you back in control.

Problem-Solving Steps

1. Identifying and Defining the Problem

The first step is to clearly identify the issue at hand. This involves understanding what the problem is and its impact on your life. Ask yourself questions like:

- What is the problem?

- How does it affect me?

2. Explore Possibilities

Once the problem is defined, brainstorm possible solutions. Consider various options and think critically about the potential consequences of each. Evaluate the pros and cons to gain a clear perspective on which alternatives might work best.

3. Decide and Design Your Solution

After generating alternatives, assess them based on effectiveness, feasibility and potential outcomes. Choose the most suitable solution then create a detailed plan of action—including steps, resources needed and timelines.

4. Execute and Check Your Results

Execute the chosen solution according to your plan. Monitor the process and outcomes closely. Check your results to see if the problem is being resolved and make adjustments if necessary.

Set Boundaries on Your Thoughts

If a thought isn't productive, let it go. You can even set a "worry time"—a specific 10-15 minute window each day to acknowledge your concerns. Beyond that, don't entertain them. By setting limits, you train your brain to stop returning to unproductive thoughts.

IN MY CONTROL	OUT OF MY CONTROL
My thoughts	The past
How i speak to myself	The opinions of others
The goals i set	The future
How i spend my free time	What happens around me

My boundaries	What other people think of me
What i give my energy to	The outcomes of my efforts
How i handle challenges	The unexpected challenges
My actions and reactions	The actions of others

Cultivate a "Take Action" Habit

Overthinking often hides behind the mask of "I'm just being thorough." But in reality, it holds you back from action. Commit to acting on your goals even when they're not perfectly planned.

Remember, every thought is a choice, and every choice is a step forward. Free yourself from the mental clutter, and watch how your life begins to move in the direction you've always dreamed of.

75

Take a deep breath, and let it go,

Feel the weight lift, let the tension flow.

Relax your mind, release the strain,

For every storm will end, and peace will reign.

Problems are temporary, just passing through,

Hold on to hope, strength will renew.

Take a deep breath, trust in your way,

And know that calm will find its way.

15

Battling Self-Doubt

*"Your mind is a garden. Your thoughts are the seeds.
You can grow flowers or you can grow weeds."*

The inner critic, a persistent and often merciless voice, can cripple our confidence and hinder our progress. Self-doubt, its primary weapon, can infiltrate every aspect of our lives, from personal relationships to professional endeavours. Recognising and understanding the inner critic is crucial to overcoming self-doubt and unlocking our true potential.

What is Self-doubt?

Self-doubt is the nagging feeling of uncertainty and inadequacy that erodes our confidence. It's the voice that whispers:

- You're not good enough
- You'll never succeed
- You're not worthy

Self-doubt can manifest in various forms:

1. Fear of failure

2. Perfectionism

3. Procrastination

4. Comparison to others

The Inner Critic: Who is it?

The inner critic is the part of our psyche that perpetuates self-doubt. It's a collection of negative thoughts, emotions and experiences that shape our self-perception.

To overcome self-doubt, we must first recognise the inner critic's presence.

Common Signs of the Inner Critic

1. Negative self-talk

2. Self-Blame

3. Procrastination

4. Difficulty receiving compliments

5. Self-comparison

6. Perfectionism

7. Fear of failure

To overcome self-doubt, we must:

1. Acknowledge the inner critic's presence

2. Challenge negative thoughts

3. Practice self-compassion

4. Focus on strengths

5. Develop a growth mindset

6. Cultivate self-awareness

7. Reframe failure as learning

Reclaiming Your Inner strength

1. Identify your values and strengths

2. Set realistic goals

3. Celebrate small victories

4. Practice gratitude

5. Surround yourself with positive influences

Recognising and understanding the inner critic is the first step towards conquering self-doubt. By acknowledging its presence and motivations, we can begin to challenge negative thoughts and cultivate self-compassion.

Remember, the inner critic is not a reflection of your worth; it's a distorted lens through which you view yourself.

Identifying Negative Self-talk Patterns

Negative self-talk patterns can be detrimental to our mental health, self-esteem and overall well-being. Recognising these patterns is the first step towards changing them.

Common negative self-talk patterns:

1. All-or-nothing thinking: I'm a complete failure.

2. Catastrophizing: This is a disaster.

3. Overgeneralization: I always mess up.

4. Personalization: It's all my fault.

5. Mind Reading: They think I'm stupid.

6. Should Statements: I should have done better.

7. Labelling: I'm a loser.

8. Blame-shifting: It's their fault.

9. Perfectionism: I must be perfect.

10. Rumination: Dwelling on negative thoughts.

Challenging Negative Self-talk:

1. Reality-check: Is this thought based on facts? Is it rational?

2. Reframe: Replace negative thoughts with positive ones.

3. Focus on strengths: Turn your weaknesses into the strength of unwavering focus.

4. Practice self compassion: Replacing harsh self-criticism with understanding and kindness.

5. Develop a growth mindset: Transforms negative self-talk into opportunities for learning and self-improvement.

Replacing Negative Self-talk with positive affirmations:

1. I'm capable and competent.

2. I learn from my mistakes.

3. I'm worthy of love and respect.

4. I can handle challenges.

5. I'm grateful for my strengths.

When shadows rise and fears take hold,

Remember, strength lies in the bold.

Doubt may whisper, "you're not enough"

But trust your heart, though the road is tough.

Each step forward, though filled with fear,

Brings you closer, the path made clear.

Believe in yourself, let courage shout—

YOU ARE THE LIGHT THAT DROWNS THE DOUBT.

16

Healthy Body, Healthy Mind

*"The mind and body are not separate.
What affects one, affects the other."*

In today's world, we often separate physical health from mental well-being, assuming that one can be nurtured without the other. But the body and mind are intertwined in ways that make it nearly impossible to nurture one without affecting the other. This chapter dives into the powerful relationship between a healthy body and a healthy mind—and how simple, consistent choices can create a ripple effect for a balanced and fulfilling life.

The Science of Body-Mind Connection

Imagine you're a car owner. To keep your car running smoothly, you wouldn't just take care of the engine and ignore the tires or fuel it but skip oil changes. Your body and mind work similarly—each affects the other. The mind communicates with the body through complex neural and hormonal pathways, influencing everything from energy levels to emotional stability. When we neglect physical health, the mind pays the price in mental fatigue, increased stress and poor emotional regulation. But when we care for our body, our mind is better equipped to stay focused, positive and resilient.

Movement as a Mental Health Tool

Take Suhani, for example, a 35-year-old working mom of two who struggled with mood swings and stress. She rarely made time for exercise, feeling too drained after her long days. But she decided to start small by taking a 15-minute walk each morning. Over time, she noticed not only a boost in her energy but also fewer moments of irritability. Physical activity releases endorphins and serotonin—chemicals that naturally improve mood and reduce anxiety. For Suhani, going for a morning walk became a mental escape, allowing her to process thoughts and return to her family with a fresh, positive outlook.

Nutrition: Fuel for the Mind

Consider Raj, a software developer, who relied on processed snacks and energy drinks to power through late nights at work. Though convenient, his diet left him feeling sluggish and mentally foggy. Realising the toll on his health, Raj gradually shifted to a diet of whole foods, incorporating more fruits, vegetables and proteins. Within weeks, he noticed fewer afternoon slumps, improved focus and a steadier mood. Foods rich in nutrients, like leafy greens, lean proteins and nuts, help nourish the brain and stabilise emotions, while hydration keeps energy consistent and the mind alert.

Sleep: The Brain's Reset Button

Bhavya, a college student, used to think she could compensate for sleepless nights by drinking more coffee. But frequent sleep deprivation leads to irritability, forgetfulness and anxiety. After learning how sleep affects brain function, Bhavya made changes: no screens an hour before bed and a set sleep schedule. With 7-8 hours of consistent sleep, her mind felt clearer, she handled stress better and her mood improved.

Sleep allows the brain to clear out toxins, process emotions and renew itself, directly influencing our ability to face challenges calmly and effectively.

Mindfulness and Relaxation Practices

Ayaan, a corporate manager, often felt overwhelmed by work demands and personal responsibilities. He noticed that his stress not only affected his mind but also took a toll on his physical health, causing headaches and tension. Taking a friend's suggestion, Ayaan tried five minutes of deep breathing each morning. Over time, this simple mindfulness practice helped him feel more centred and manage stress more easily.

Mindfulness strengthens mental resilience, teaching us to focus on the present moment and release tension—essential skills in today's high-stress world.

17

Acceptance and Peace

"Peace is found when we accept what was, forgive what hurt, and let go of what binds us."

Life is full of unexpected twists, setbacks and pressures that test our ability to cope. From career challenges to personal hardships, these moments can make us feel overwhelmed or even defeated. But mental resilience—the ability to recover, adapt and grow through adversity—is a powerful skill that enables us to not only withstand these challenges but emerge stronger and wiser.

Building resilience isn't about avoiding hardships; it's about learning how to respond to them with a mindset that promotes growth rather than fear or frustration. Like a muscle, resilience strengthens with practice and intentional effort. The more we work on it, the better we become at handling stress, managing setbacks and finding solutions, regardless of the obstacles in our path.

Acceptance is a crucial tool in overcoming self-imposed barriers. Often, we struggle because we resist reality. We fight against the truth of our circumstances, wishing things were different, blaming ourselves or others for what went wrong. But this resistance only drains our energy and keeps us stuck in a cycle of frustration. Acceptance, on the other hand, allows us to see things clearly and frees us to take action from a place of clarity.

Accepting Yourself

The first step in acceptance is learning to accept yourself. This means embracing who you are right now, with all your strengths and weaknesses. Too often, we are our own harshest critics, holding ourselves to unrealistic standards of perfection. But growth doesn't come from self-criticism; it comes from self-compassion. When you accept yourself fully—acknowledging your flaws and mistakes without letting them define you—you give yourself the freedom to improve and grow.

Self-acceptance is about understanding that you are a work in progress. No one is perfect and it's okay to be flawed. By accepting yourself, you lay the foundation for building self-confidence, resilience and peace of mind. You start to realise that your worth isn't tied to perfection but to your willingness to learn and grow.

Accepting Circumstances

Life doesn't always go the way we plan. Setbacks, failures and unforeseen challenges are inevitable, and while we can't control every aspect of life, we can control how we respond to it. Acceptance of circumstances is about acknowledging reality for what it is—without denying it or wishing it away. This doesn't mean you have to like or agree with everything that happens but it does mean recognising that some things are outside of your control.

When you accept what is happening in your life, you stop wasting energy resisting or blaming. Instead, you focus on what you can control—your attitude, your actions and how you move forward. Acceptance gives you the power to take responsibility for your next steps rather than getting stuck in the past or worrying about the future.

Acceptance as a Path to Peace

Acceptance leads to inner peace. When you stop fighting against the things you cannot change—whether it's your past, your limitations or life's uncertainties—you free yourself from unnecessary suffering. This sense of peace doesn't mean giving up on your goals or ambitions; it means approaching life from a place of calm and clarity rather than from frustration or desperation.

In accepting yourself and your circumstances, you open the door to real growth. You begin to understand that while you can't control everything, you have the power to change yourself, your mindset and your actions. And that's where true transformation begins.

The 3 As: Avoid, Alter and Accept

Life often presents us with challenges that can feel overwhelming. When faced with difficult situations, it's easy to feel stuck or helpless. However, by applying the 3 A's—Avoid, Alter and Accept—you can find clarity and take control of how you respond to life's obstacles. These three strategies offer a practical approach to handling adversity and moving forward.

Avoid the Situation

Sometimes, the best solution is to simply avoid a situation that brings negativity or harm. This doesn't mean running away from responsibilities or ignoring problems, but rather, setting boundaries and making conscious choices about what you let into your life. If something is not serving your well-being—whether it's toxic relationships, unhealthy environments or unnecessary stress—you have the power to avoid it. Avoidance helps you protect your energy and focus on what truly matters.

Alter the Situation

When avoidance isn't possible, the next step is to alter the situation. This means looking for ways to change the dynamics of the challenge you are facing. Can you communicate more effectively? Can you approach the problem from a different angle? Altering is about taking action, finding solutions and adjusting your approach to create a better outcome. It empowers you to shift your perspective and transform what feels unchangeable.

Accept the Situation

If avoiding or altering the situation isn't an option, acceptance is the final and most powerful step. Acceptance means acknowledging reality as it is, without resistance. While it might seem difficult, accepting a situation allows you to let go of the emotional burden it creates. Acceptance is not giving up—it's about recognising what you cannot change and focusing your energy on what you can control: your attitude and response.

Venting and Releasing Emotions

Bottling up emotions can have a detrimental impact on mental health. When we keep our feelings inside, they can build up, leading to stress, anxiety and even physical symptoms like headaches or fatigue. Venting—whether it's talking to a trusted friend, journaling or engaging in creative expression—allows you to release pent-up emotions in a healthy way.

Sometimes, it's okay to acknowledge that things aren't perfect and to share how you feel. It's a necessary release that helps clear the mental clutter and allows you to move forward with a lighter, more focused mindset. Finding safe spaces and methods to express your emotions is vital for your mental well-being.

Self-love

Self-love involves recognising your inherent worth and treating yourself with kindness and compassion. By shifting your internal dialogue from self-criticism to acceptance, you empower yourself to accept both your strengths and vulnerabilities. This shift not only enhances your emotional stability and confidence but also fosters resilience, enabling you to navigate life's challenges with greater ease. When you prioritise self-love, you create a safe space for healing and exploration, allowing you to cultivate a positive mindset that propels you forward.

Moreover, self-love profoundly impacts your relationships with others. When you value yourself, you establish healthy boundaries and make choices that align with your true aspiration, leading to deeper connections and a more fulfilling life.

So, love yourself the way you are.

Hope

Hope is a powerful force in maintaining mental wellness. It gives us something to hold on to during difficult times, reminding us that there is a brighter future ahead, even when the present feels overwhelming. Cultivating hope involves maintaining a positive outlook, setting goals and believing that challenges are temporary. Hope is what pushes us forward when we feel like giving up.

Forgiveness

Equally important is forgiveness—both for yourself and others. Holding onto grudges or regrets can weigh heavily on your mind, leading to prolonged emotional distress. Learning to forgive doesn't mean forgetting or condoning harmful behaviour; it means freeing yourself from the emotional burden of resentment. By forgiving, you release the mental tension that keeps you stuck in the past, allowing you to focus on your present and future well-being.

"Forgive people, not because they deserve forgiveness but because you deserve peace."

Gratitude

Gratitude is a profound practice that significantly enhances mental wellness by shifting our focus from what we lack to what we have. In a world often dominated by comparison and discontent, taking the time to appreciate our lives can create a powerful sense of fulfilment. Many individuals dream of the lives we often take for granted yet the reality of our existence—our health, our experiences and the simple act of being alive—is a gift worth acknowledging. When feelings of envy or inadequacy arise, a moment of reflection on what we are grateful for can shift our perspective and foster a more positive mindset.

Rather than getting caught up in comparing ourselves to others, we can cultivate an attitude of gratitude by recognising the many blessings in our lives. This practice extends beyond our relationships, careers or material possessions; it encompasses the fundamental aspects of our existence, such as the ability to breathe, the beauty of a sunrise, nature or the feeling of a gentle breeze touching our skin. Acknowledging these simple joys reminds us of our worth and encourages us to engage in life with intention. By focusing on gratitude, we empower ourselves to live more meaningfully, finding joy in the present moment and taking steps to create a life that reflects our values and aspirations. Ultimately, gratitude fosters resilience and positivity, guiding us toward a more fulfilling and enriched life.

Your Mental Wellness, Your Responsibility

At the end of the day, no one else can prioritise your well-being for you. Your mental health is as important as your physical health and both require your attention and care.

Your well-being is your responsibility and by making the conscious choice to take care of yourself mentally and emotionally, you create the foundation for a resilient, fulfilled and empowered life. It all starts with you.

Pathway to Peace

In the heart of acceptance, we find our release

Letting go of the burdens, inviting in peace.

With open arms, we acknowledge what's true,

*Transforming our struggles, allowing hope to break
through.*

Hope is a whisper that calls us to rise,

A beacon of light in the darkest of skies.

It nurtures our dreams and fuels our desires,

In the warmth of its glow, our spirits aspire.

Forgiveness, a remedy that heals wounds of the past,

Releasing the weight, our freedom is cast.

With gratitude flowing like a river so wide,

We cherish our journey, with kindness as our guide.

18

The Power of Positive Thinking

"The happiness of your life depends upon the quality of your thoughts."

~ Marcus Aurelius

In a world often dominated by negativity and doubt, the power of positive thinking emerges as a transformative force. It is not merely about wearing rose-coloured glasses or ignoring life's challenges; rather, it is about cultivating an optimistic mindset that empowers you to navigate adversity, enhance your well-being and achieve your goals.

Positive thinking is the practice of focusing on the good in any situation. It involves adopting an optimistic outlook, expecting favourable outcomes and believing in your ability to overcome obstacles. While it may seem simple, this mental shift can have profound effects on your emotional and physical health.

Research shows that positive thinkers tend to experience lower levels of stress, improved immune function, and a greater overall sense of well-being. They are more resilient in the face of challenges, able to bounce back from setbacks with renewed energy and determination. Positive thinking isn't about denial; it's about acknowledging difficulties while maintaining hope and a proactive approach to solutions.

The Science Behind Positive Thinking

The impact of positive thinking extends beyond mere emotions; it influences our brains and bodies in remarkable ways. When you engage in positive thinking, your brain releases neurotransmitters like dopamine and serotonin, which promote feelings of happiness and reduce stress. Studies have shown that optimistic individuals are more likely to engage in healthy behaviours, have better coping strategies and enjoy longer, healthier lives.

Moreover, positive thinking can enhance your problem-solving abilities. When you maintain an optimistic mindset, you are more open to creative solutions and new possibilities. This approach encourages you to tackle challenges head-on rather than feeling defeated by them.

Techniques to Cultivate Positive Thinking

While positive thinking can come naturally to some, it is a skill that can be developed through practice. Here are effective techniques to help you harness the power of positive thinking:

- **Practice Gratitude:** Regularly reflect on the things you are grateful for in your life. This simple practice can shift your focus from what is lacking to what is abundant, fostering a positive outlook.

- **Challenge Negative Thoughts:** Pay attention to your internal dialogue. When negative thoughts arise, challenge them by asking yourself if they are accurate or if there is another way to view the situation. Replace negative affirmations with positive ones that reflect your true potential.

- **Surround Yourself with Positivity:** The people you interact with can influence your mindset. Surround yourself with supportive and positive individuals who uplift and inspire you. Engage in communities or activities that promote positivity and encouragement.

- **Visualise Success:** Spend time visualising your goals and the steps you need to take to achieve them. Imagine yourself succeeding and enjoying the outcomes. Visualisation can reinforce your belief in your abilities and help you approach challenges with confidence.

"What you think, you become. What you feel, you attract. What you imagine, you create."

~ Buddha

- **Engage in Positive Self-Talk:** Be mindful of your self-talk. Replace self-criticism with supportive and encouraging language. Instead of saying, "I can't do this," try affirming, "I am capable, and I will find a way."

- **Limit Negative Influences:** Identify and limit exposure to negative influences whether from news, social media or pessimistic individuals. Seek out uplifting content such as motivational podcasts, books or affirmations.

- **Focus on Solutions:** When faced with challenges, shift your focus from the problem to potential solutions. Ask yourself what steps you can take to address the issue rather than dwelling on the obstacles.

Overcoming Obstacles to Positive Thinking

Despite the benefits of positive thinking, obstacles may arise that challenge your ability to maintain an optimistic outlook. These can include stress, fear of failure or past experiences. It's essential to acknowledge these barriers without letting them dictate your mindset.

Let's have a look at the two simple approaches that can help you eradicate any obstacles.

- **Recognize and Accept Emotions:** It's okay to feel negative emotions. Instead of suppressing them, acknowledge and accept them. Understanding that negative feelings are a natural part of life can help you release their hold on you and refocus on positive aspects.

- **Reframe Challenges:** View challenges as opportunities for growth rather than threats. This shift in perspective can transform your approach to adversity, making it easier to maintain a positive outlook.

Harnessing the power of positive thinking is a journey that requires intentional practice and dedication. By adopting an optimistic mindset, you can transform your approach to challenges, enhance your well-being and unlock your true potential.

"The greatest weapon against stress is our ability to choose one thought over another."

Now sit back and enjoy the story of Khushi and her power of optimistic endeavours.

Khushi was a bright and imaginative girl known for her infectious laughter and vibrant energy. However, life had a way of challenging her spirit. She lived in a bustling town filled with a mix of opportunities and obstacles. As she entered her teenage years, Khushi began to feel the weight of negativity that surrounded her.

Her friends, once supportive, started to fall into the habit of complaining about everything. They often talked about how difficult life was, how nothing ever went right and how they were stuck in a rut. Khushi, wanting to fit in, started to adopt this pessimistic mindset. Gradually, she found herself echoing their sentiments. "Nothing good ever happens to me," she would say. "I'm just not lucky."

As she focused on the negatives, her life began to reflect her thoughts. Her grades slipped as she lost interest in studying. She avoided extracurricular activities, feeling as though she wouldn't succeed at anything. Opportunities for new friendships and experiences passed by her, and once a joyful girl, she now began to feel trapped in a cycle of gloom.

One day, while wandering through a local park, Khushi stumbled upon a small art exhibition. Colourful paintings adorned the walls, each telling a unique story of hope, joy and perseverance. As she walked through the exhibit, one painting caught her eye—a stunning landscape of a sunrise breaking through dark clouds. The vibrant colours filled her with warmth and hope, reminding her of the beauty that still existed in the world.

Inspired, Khushi sat on a nearby bench and began to reflect on her life. She thought about how she had let negativity cloud her perspective. At that moment, she made a decision. She would no longer allow negative thoughts to dictate her reality. Instead, she would seek out positivity and embrace the good in her life.

The very next day, Khushi started a new routine. She began each morning by writing down three things she was grateful for. At first, it felt challenging to find anything positive, but as she continued, she discovered small joys—like the beauty of nature, a compliment from a stranger or the warmth of the sun on her face. With each new day, her list grew longer and she felt lighter.

Khushi also began to change her self-talk. Whenever negative thoughts crept in, she countered them with affirmations. "I am capable. Good things are coming my way. I can create my own happiness." Slowly, she started to notice a shift in her outlook. Instead of feeling defeated, she felt empowered.

With her newfound positivity, Khushi decided to take on challenges she had previously avoided. She joined the art club at school, channelling her feelings into her artwork. She discovered a passion for painting and began to express her emotions through vibrant colours and captivating scenes. Her artwork soon caught the attention of her teachers and they encouraged her to enter a regional art competition.

Feeling excited but nervous, Khushi put her heart into creating a piece that represented her journey from darkness to light. The day of the competition arrived and as she stood among her peers, she felt a rush of confidence. Regardless of the outcome, she had embraced her passion and transformed her mindset.

When the winners were announced, Khushi was overwhelmed with joy when her name was called out as a winner. As she accepted her award, she realised that her journey was not just about winning; it was about adapting the power of positivity.

Khushi's transformation inspired her friends. They began to notice the change in her and asked what had happened. With enthusiasm, she shared her journey of gratitude and positivity. They were intrigued and wanted to try it themselves. Slowly, the group began to shift their conversations from complaints to discussions about their goals and dreams.

Together, they practised gratitude and encouraged each other to pursue their passions. As they fostered a more positive environment, they began to see improvements in their own lives. One by one, they started to find their own strengths and successes, proving that positivity was contagious.

In time, Khushi became a beacon of hope in her community. She organised workshops and art sessions to help others discover the power of positive thinking. The group, once filled with negativity, began to transform into a place where dreams flourished and aspirations took flight.

Khushi learned that while challenges would always be a part of life, her attitude could change her experience. By adapting positivity, she unlocked the door to a world filled with possibilities, proving that when you change your thoughts, you truly can change your life.

Cultivating positivity is a journey that takes time. Instant results are rare, and it's important to be patient with yourself as you navigate this process. Accepting the idea that change will happen gradually allows you to stay motivated and focused on the long-term benefits of a positive mindset.

Utilise the power of positive thinking, and let it illuminate your path as you navigate life's ups and downs. As you cultivate positivity within yourself, you'll find that the world around you begins to shift in extraordinary ways.

A whisper of light in shadows cast,
A gentle strength that holds you fast.
In every challenge, it finds a way,
To turn the night into a brighter day.
It colours the world with hope anew,
See the beauty in all you do.
Positivity plants seeds in hearts that believe,
Nurturing dreams and helping them weave.

19

Setting Boundaries for Mental Health

"Boundaries are the distance at which I can love you and me simultaneously."

— Prentis Hemphill

In our busy and often overwhelming lives, it's easy to lose sight of our own needs. Setting boundaries is not about shutting others out but rather about creating space to protect your mental and emotional well-being. Boundaries are essential for maintaining a healthy balance in life, allowing us to engage with the world around us while safeguarding our inner peace. When we set boundaries, we honour ourselves, protect our energy and create the space we need to grow, heal and thrive.

Why Do Boundaries Matter?

There are four major reasons to understand the relevance of setting boundaries.

1. **Prevent Burnout and Exhaustion:** Constantly giving without limits leads to exhaustion. Boundaries create space for rest and replenishment.

2. **Safeguard Emotional Well-being:** By limiting toxic interactions, boundaries help preserve our mental clarity and emotional stability.

3. **Foster Healthy Relationships:** When we set boundaries, we teach others how to respect us, cultivating mutual respect and understanding.

4. **Encourage Self-care and Prioritisation:** Boundaries remind us that our needs matter and that it's okay to take time for ourselves.

Types of Boundaries

Boundaries vary depending upon the needs and situation. It can be classified into four parameters as you can read below:

1. Physical Boundaries

These include personal space, touch and the need for privacy. It's vital to communicate your need for physical space whether it's for rest or to avoid overstimulation.

2. Emotional Boundaries

These protect us from emotional labour, manipulation or toxic behaviour. It's about knowing what is emotionally draining and protecting ourselves from harmful interactions.

3. Digital Boundaries

In today's interconnected world, setting limits on our digital interactions is crucial. This could mean limiting time on social media, establishing phone call hours or not engaging in online arguments.

4. Energetic Boundaries

These protect our energy from being drained by demanding

people or situations. Learning to say no to energy-zapping commitments is a key aspect of self-care.

Boundary-Setting

Boundary setting is the art of protecting your peace while fostering mutual respect in relationships. It's about creating space for your needs, valuing your limits and communicating them clearly to others.

- I'm not available for that.

  Simple and to the point, this statement protects your time and energy without over-explaining.

- I need space, please respect my privacy.

  A respectful way to ask for the physical or emotional distance you need without any guilt.

- I prioritise my own needs.

  This reinforces your commitment to self-care and reminds others that you value your well-being.

  Setting boundaries is not a sign of weakness or selfishness. It is, in fact, an act of self-respect and a vital component of good mental health. When we set boundaries, we:

  - **Reclaim Our Energy and Time:** We stop giving away our precious resources to people or situations that drain us.

  - **Nurture Positive Relationships:** Healthy boundaries ensure that our relationships are based on respect, trust and mutual care.

  - **Cultivate Self-love and Resilience:** By

valuing ourselves enough to set limits, we build resilience against stress and emotional exhaustion.

Action Plan

Below are some simple techniques to help you in setting boundaries.

- **Identify One Area for Boundary-Setting:** It could be a relationship, a work situation or an aspect of your digital life. Start small and focus on one area where you need to establish a boundary.

- **Communicate Boundaries Clearly:** Be assertive, not aggressive. Whether it's in a conversation or a written message, clearly state your needs.

- **Practice Self-care Daily:** Regular self-care routines will help reinforce your boundaries. Prioritise activities that nurture your mind, body and spirit.

- **Review and Adjust Boundaries Regularly:** As life changes so should your boundaries. Periodically reassess your limits and adjust them as needed.

Setting boundaries is not just about protecting your space; it's about creating a life where you thrive. When you honour your own needs and communicate them effectively, you're giving yourself the gift of mental and emotional freedom. And in doing so, you not only protect your well-being but also lay the foundation for deeper, more fulfilling connections with others. Remember, you are worthy of respect and your mental health deserves to be prioritised.

"Set your boundaries, protect your peace"

PART FOUR

Taking Actions and
Responsibilities

20

Turning Intentions into Actions

"Vision without execution is hallucination."

~ Thomas Edison

In the journey of personal growth, the gap between dreams and reality often comes down to one critical factor—execution. We all have goals, aspirations and ideas that hold the potential for transformation. Yet, many find themselves stuck in a cycle of intention without action. This chapter delves into the art of execution, providing you with powerful strategies to take meaningful actions that bridge the gap between what you desire and what you achieve.

Execution is not merely about doing; it's about doing with intention and purpose. It involves taking the necessary steps to bring your plans to fruition. Here's why execution is crucial:

1. Turning Ideas into Reality

Ideas are merely potential until they are acted upon. Execution transforms concepts into tangible outcomes, allowing you to manifest your vision.

2. Building Momentum

Action creates momentum. Each step you take propels you forward, making it easier to continue moving toward your goals. Conversely, inaction can lead to stagnation.

3. Learning Through Doing

The process of execution offers invaluable lessons. Even if things don't go as planned, each experience provides insights that refine your approach, making you more adept for future challenges.

Strategies for Effective Execution

- **Set Clear and Specific Goals**

  When goals are well-defined, they become actionable, measurable and motivating, making it easier to track progress and stay focused on achieving your desired outcome.

- **Break Goals into Actionable Steps**

  Large goals can be daunting. Break them down into smaller, manageable tasks. This not only makes the process less intimidating but also allows you to track your progress more easily.

- **Create a Timeline**

  Setting deadlines for each task adds a sense of urgency and accountability. A timeline helps you prioritise your actions and ensures that you stay on track.

- **Establish a Routine**

  Create a daily or weekly routine that incorporates time for executing your action plan. Consistency is the key; making your goals a regular part of your life increases the likelihood of success.

- **Eliminate Distractions**

  Identify and minimise distractions that hinder your ability to take action. This could involve setting boundaries around social media usage, creating a designated workspace or using productivity tools.

- **Cultivate an Execution Mindset**

  Develop a mindset that embraces action over perfection. Understand that progress is often messy and non-linear. Focus on making strides toward your goals rather than waiting for the perfect moment.

- **Utilise Visualisation Techniques**

  Visualising your success can enhance motivation and clarify your path. Spend time imagining the positive outcomes of your actions and consider the steps needed to get there.

- **Seek Accountability Partners**

  Share your goals with someone who can hold you accountable. This could be a friend, mentor or coach. Regular check-ins with your accountability partner can motivate you to stay committed to your actions.

- **Reflect and Adjust**

  After taking action, take time to reflect on the outcomes. What worked? What didn't? Use this reflection to adjust your strategies and improve future execution.

Overcoming Obstacles to Execution

Even with the best strategies in place, obstacles will arise.

It's essential to anticipate potential challenges and develop resilience in the face of setbacks. So, how to overcome any obstacles? Read on.

1. Manage Fear of Failure

Fear of failure can be paralysing. Reframe your perspective. View failure as a learning opportunity rather than a setback. Embrace the idea that each misstep brings you closer to success.

2. Combat Perfectionism

Perfectionism can stall execution. Understand that perfection is an illusion; what matters is progress. Allow yourself to take imperfect action, knowing that you can refine your approach as you go.

3. Stay Flexible and Adaptable

Life is unpredictable and plans may need to change. Stay adaptable and be willing to modify your strategies when faced with new information or challenges.

Mastering the execution is about taking meaningful actions that align with your goals. It requires clarity, commitment and resilience. As you implement the strategies outlined in this chapter, remember that execution is a skill that can be developed over time.

Embrace the journey and stay focused on your vision. By mastering the art of execution, you can turn your aspirations into reality and create the life you truly desire.

Remember, the only limit to your success is your willingness to take action. So, take that step today and ignite the change you seek.

Implementation is Difficult

You may have read many books on self-help but the art of execution is something only you can practise. Believe me, if you follow the steps outlined here, you can achieve your goals.

The Art of Execution

In the quiet dawn, where dreams take flight,
Lies the art of execution, bold and bright.
Intentions whisper, a gentle breeze,
But action, my friend, brings them to their knees.
Embrace the discomfort, the challenges rise,
For in facing the struggle, true courage lies.
With faith as your compass and passion as fuel,
You'll turn visions to reality, break every rule.
So paint with conviction, let your heart guide,
In the dance of execution, let purpose collide.
For every masterpiece starts with a spark,
It's the art of execution that ignites the dark.

21

Facing Challenges Head-on

"The greatest glory in living lies not in never falling, but in rising every time we fall."

– Nelson Mandela

Life is full of challenges—big and small, personal and professional, expected and unforeseen. No one is exempt from hardship. The true test lies not in the challenges themselves but in how we face them. Do we let fear, doubt or the weight of uncertainty defeat us or do we rise to meet them head-on, embracing them as opportunities for growth and transformation?

To face challenges head-on, we must first acknowledge that they are a natural part of life. They may disrupt our sense of comfort, they may shake us to the core but they also serve as the catalyst for our greatest growth. When we embrace the fight within, we tap into a powerful resource: resilience.

The Art of Resilience

Resilience is not about being immune to life's difficulties; it's about having the strength and flexibility to withstand them. It's the courage to continue despite the odds, to rise after every fall, and to remain steadfast in the face of adversity. Resilience is the ability to bend without breaking, to adapt, and to become stronger with each challenge faced. It is not just a trait, but a skill that can be cultivated.

To build resilience, we must reframe our perception of challenges. Rather than seeing them as insurmountable obstacles, we must begin to see them as opportunities for growth. Every challenge is a chance to become better, to push past our limits, and to develop qualities like patience, perseverance, and grit.

Challenges come in many forms but they can be broadly categorised into three types:

- **Internal Challenges:** These are the battles within us. Self-doubt, fear, procrastination and negative self-talk are some of the most common internal challenges we face. These are the obstacles that hold us back from reaching our full potential. Overcoming these requires cultivating self-awareness, challenging negative thoughts and developing a mindset of self-compassion and confidence.

- **External Challenges:** These are the circumstances and situations we face in the world around us— financial struggles, relationship issues, health problems and career obstacles. While we cannot always control these external forces, we can control how we respond. The key to overcoming external challenges is taking proactive steps, seeking solutions and maintaining focus on what we can control.

- **Existential Challenges:** These are the big, deep questions of life:
  - What is my purpose?
  - What is the meaning of my life?

These challenges are not always easy to face but they are essential for personal growth. To tackle existential challenges, we must be willing to reflect, explore and connect with our core values and beliefs. It's through this process that we gain clarity on our life's purpose.

The 5-Step Challenge-Conquering Framework

Facing challenges head-on requires a structured approach. The following 5-step framework will help you tackle obstacles effectively:

1. **Acknowledge:** The first step is to fully acknowledge the challenge. Avoid denial or avoidance. Recognise the impact of the challenge on your life and emotions. This is the moment of acceptance—facing the reality of the situation.

2. **Assess:** Once you've acknowledged the challenge, take a step back and evaluate its severity. What is at stake? What are your options? Assess the challenge by breaking it down into manageable parts. This helps reduce overwhelm and gives you a clear view of potential solutions.

3. **Accept:** Embrace the challenge as an opportunity for growth. Challenges are rarely comfortable, but by accepting them, you shift your mindset from one of resistance to one of action. Understand that overcoming this challenge will require effort, but it will also lead to personal growth.

4. **Act:** This is the most important step—taking action. Develop a plan and start moving forward. Even small steps will make a difference. Don't wait for the perfect time; act now. Progress, no matter how small, builds momentum.

5. **Adjust:** Flexibility is the key. Not everything will go as planned, and that's okay. Be prepared to adjust your approach as needed. If one solution doesn't work, try another. Resilience is about adapting, not stubbornly sticking to a single course of action.

Mindset Shifts

A shift in mindset—from seeing obstacles as roadblocks to viewing them as opportunities for growth—can transform the way you navigate life's adversities.

- **From Victim to Victor:** Life happens to everyone but how you respond makes all the difference. Instead of seeing yourself as a victim of circumstances, take ownership of your situation. Recognise that you have the power to choose your response and to take control of your future.

- **From Fear to Courage:** Fear is a natural response to challenges but it doesn't have to dictate your actions. Courage is not the absence of fear but the willingness to face it. Push through the fear, step into the unknown and trust yourself to navigate it.

- **From Doubt to Confidence:** Self-doubt is a barrier that prevents us from reaching our potential. Transform doubt into confidence by focusing on your strengths and past successes. Trust in your ability to handle whatever comes your way.

- **From Comfort to Growth:** Growth happens outside of your comfort zone. Embrace discomfort as a sign that you're stretching your limits and becoming more resilient. The pain of growth is temporary but the rewards are lifelong.

Life moves onward through each hurdles;

It's a journey you control—

Will you accept the pain and lessons,

Or let them take a toll?

You can choose to change your course

And find new ways to cope,

Or let the weight of worry crush your

Heart and dim your hope.

22

Taking Responsibility for Your Choices

"You are the architect of your own life; you can build it up or tear it down with the choices you make."

Taking responsibility for your choices is one of the most empowering steps you can take in life. It's the moment you decide to stop being a passive observer and instead become the architect of your own journey. Responsibility isn't about blame or perfection—it's about owning the path you're on, learning from every decision and steering yourself toward the person you want to be.

When you embrace responsibility, you acknowledge that your life is a product of your choices. You gain the freedom to shape your own reality, to learn from your setbacks and to create a future aligned with your values and goals.

The Importance of Responsibility

Owning your choices means you're accountable not only for your successes but also for your mistakes. This mindset builds resilience, helping you learn from setbacks rather than being weighed down by them. Responsibility is not about being perfect; it's about making thoughtful, value-aligned choices that reflect who you are and who you want to become.

Breaking the Blame Cycle

By taking responsibility, you break the cycle of blaming circumstances or others. Instead of feeling stuck, you focus on what you can control. This shift brings greater clarity, allowing you to move forward constructively and make meaningful changes.

Steps to take on Responsibility

1. **Reflect Honestly:** Examine your past decisions without judgement to see where you can grow.

2. **Set Purposeful Intentions:** Make choices that align with your core values and goals.

3. **Accept and Learn from Mistakes:** Treat missteps as learning experiences rather than failures.

4. **Focus on Action:** Replace blame with actionable steps that lead to improvement.

Taking responsibility for your choices means recognising that every decision shapes your future. Whether you make a good life or destroy it, the power—and responsibility—rests with you. Each choice you make, from how you handle setbacks to the goals you pursue, either builds you up or holds you back. Blaming others or circumstances keeps you stuck; owning your actions gives you control. When you accept that your life is a reflection of your choices, you gain the power to change it. Ultimately, your life is in your hands—it's your choice, your responsibility.

You are responsible for your actions, and every choice you make shapes your future. The power lies in your hands to decide how you respond to situations, so choose wisely, as your decisions reflect your values, growth, and overall well-being.

23

The Comfort Zone Trap

A cocoon of ease where fears softly fade,

Yet outside its borders, bold adventures await.

Break free from the stillness, let courage take flight,

For life blooms in the daring, in stepping towards light.

The comfort zone is a familiar place; a mental space where you feel safe and secure. It's a zone of routine and predictability, where the risk of failure is low, but so is the potential for growth. While it might seem appealing, remaining in your comfort zone can become a trap that stifles your personal development. This chapter will explore the dangers of the comfort zone, how it limits your potential, and practical strategies to break free and embrace growth.

The comfort zone is defined by familiar behaviours, environments and mindsets that provide a sense of security. While it's natural to seek comfort, excessive reliance on this zone can lead to stagnation.

Let's look at some of the risks of staying in the comfort zone:

- **Stagnation:** Remaining in your comfort zone can lead to a lack of progress. When you avoid challenges, you miss out on valuable learning experiences that can propel you forward.

- **Fear of Change:** Prolonged comfort can create a fear of change, making it increasingly difficult to step outside your familiar boundaries. The longer you stay, the more daunting the idea of change becomes.

- **Lost Opportunities:** By avoiding discomfort, you might miss opportunities for growth whether in your career, relationships or personal endeavours. Each moment spent in comfort can be a moment lost to potential.

Now the question is how you can break free from the comfort zone trap. Here we go:

- Recognise Your Patterns

  The first step to escaping the comfort zone is recognising your habits and patterns. Are you avoiding challenges? Do you gravitate towards routine at the expense of growth?

- Set Incremental Challenges

  Challenge yourself with small, manageable tasks that push you slightly beyond your comfort zone. Gradually increasing your exposure to discomfort will build your confidence.

- Reframe Your Mindset

  Shift your perspective from viewing discomfort as something negative to seeing it as an opportunity for growth. Embrace the idea that growth often occurs outside your comfort zone.

- Create a Growth Plan

  Outline specific goals that require you to step outside your comfort zone.

- Surround Yourself with Growth-Minded Individuals

  Seek out relationships with people who encourage growth and embrace challenges. Their influence can inspire you to step out of your comfort zone.

The comfort zone trap can hinder your personal growth and potential. Remember, *It's You vs You.* The only thing standing between you and your dreams is your willingness to step outside of what feels comfortable.

Embrace discomfort as a catalyst for growth and watch as you unlock new opportunities and experiences that enrich your life. The journey beyond your comfort zone is where transformation happens--take that first step today.

> *"Comfort feels safe but holds us still,*
> *Growth awaits where fear meets will."*

Now, let's read Rohan's story.

Rohan lived in a small town with his father, surrounded by memories and familiar routines. He sat on his bed, the dim light of the room illuminated only by the flickering screen of his mobile phone. It was yet another day spent immersed in mobile games, escaping into a digital world where he could be anything but himself. Now thirty, Rohan felt the weight of his unfulfilled potential bearing down on him. He had graduated as an engineer but turned down several job offers after graduation, convinced that something better would come along.

In those early days, Rohan imagined a future filled with excitement and opportunity. He saw friends embarking on careers, finding passion in their work and forging their paths. Yet, instead of taking the plunge, Rohan chose comfort. With his father working tirelessly to provide for them, Rohan settled into a daily routine of eating, sleeping, and gaming, scrolling reels and shorts, avoiding responsibility at all costs.

"Rohan, have you thought about looking for a job?" his father would occasionally ask, concern etched on his face.

"Yeah, Dad, I'm just waiting for the right opportunity," Rohan would reply, a familiar wave of guilt washing over him.

Days turned into weeks, then months, as Rohan grew increasingly distant from reality. With no motivation to seek employment or improve his situation, he allowed himself to become an escapist, spending his time playing games rather than addressing the growing dissatisfaction in his life.

But that all changed one fateful morning. Rohan woke up to find that his mobile was not working properly and its screen shattered beyond repair. Panic surged through him; his primary source of escape was gone. He frantically searched the house for any old device but everything else was outdated and useless.

His father, who had been working long hours at a local factory, noticed Rohan's distress. "Why don't you try doing something productive today?" Mr. Mehra suggested gently. "Maybe go for a walk or catch up with Aisha. She always thought you had potential."

"Yeah, right," Rohan scoffed, feeling a bitter sting of embarrassment. Aisha had always believed in him, often encouraging him to pursue engineering jobs or explore new hobbies. But he hadn't spoken to her in years, too ashamed to face her after wasting his time.

That day, with no games to play and nothing on television to distract him, Rohan found himself isolated in his room, surrounded by memories of a life he once aspired to lead. His mind began to spiral, distorting his thoughts. Regrets and "what-ifs" flooded his consciousness. He replayed moments from his past—the job offers he rejected, the friends he had lost touch with and the dreams he had buried deep within himself.

As days passed without any digital distractions, Rohan's isolation grew. He found himself staring out of the window at the vibrant world outside, where people were living their lives and pursuing their dreams. A familiar figure caught his eye—Aisha, now a successful architect, returning from work with a smile on her face. She radiated the kind of joy that Rohan once craved and the sight triggered an intense wave of longing within him.

One evening, driven by a mix of nostalgia and regret, Rohan decided to reach out to her. He hesitated, staring at the screen of his computer, fingers hovering over the keyboard. After a few moments of deliberation, he sent a simple message: "Hey, it's been a while. How are you?"

Aisha replied almost instantly, her enthusiasm palpable through the screen. They began chatting and Rohan felt a flicker of hope rekindle within him. She shared stories about her projects, the challenges she faced and how she never gave up on her dreams, even when times were tough.

Their conversation sparked something deep within Rohan. As he listened to Aisha, he began to realise that the comfort zone he had built was not protecting him; it was suffocating him. He felt the urge to break free and reclaim his life, to stop regretting and start living.

The next day, Rohan took a bold step. He dusted off his resume and started applying for engineering jobs, determined to overcome his fears. The process wasn't easy; he faced rejection after rejection but with each "no," he felt a little more alive.

Over time, Rohan secured a job at a local engineering firm. It was not the dream job he had envisioned but it was a start. As he walked into the office on his first day, a mix of nerves and excitement washed over him. He remembered Aisha's words: "Just take the first step and everything else will follow."

As he settled into his new role, Rohan realised that breaking free from his comfort zone was a continuous journey. He learned to accept challenges, reconnect with friends and even found joy in the small victories. No longer an escapist, he began to craft a future filled with promise.

Rohan's journey illustrates the stark reality of the comfort zone trap. It shows how easy it is to fall into complacency and the importance of taking action, even when it feels daunting. With determination and support, Rohan discovered that the path to fulfilment begins with the courage to step outside one's comfort zone and embrace life's uncertainties.

Comfort is the Enemy

It whispers lies of ease, lulls you into stagnation and steals your ambition. Progress doesn't live in comfort—it is born in discomfort, in the moments that stretch you beyond your limits. Comfort keeps you in the familiar, but greatness demands risk, struggle and pain. Every time you choose comfort, you choose to stay the same. But growth? Growth thrives in the discomfort, in the chaos, in the moments that scare you. Step out of your comfort zone or stay trapped in mediocrity. The choice is yours.

24

Learning from Mistakes and Failures

*"From every fall, a lesson learned,
In shattered hopes, new strength is earned."*

In life's grand journey, failure often feels like a dead-end, a brutal reminder of the risks we've taken and the challenges we've faced. But what if I told you that failure is not the end? That failure, instead, is one of the most powerful tools for growth, transformation and ultimately, success?

The Nature of Failure: It's Not What You Think

Most of us have been conditioned to fear failure. We associate it with weakness, defeat or lack of ability. But failure is a natural part of any process. Consider some of the world's greatest innovators and leaders—every one of them failed, often multiple times, before achieving success. Failure is not an indication of who you are but rather a signal for where you can grow.

Reframing Failure

It's not a reflection of your character; it's a result of your current strategy. By adjusting your approach and learning from the experience, you can shift failure into progress.

Think about Thomas Edison who failed 1000 times before inventing the lightbulb. When asked about it, he famously said, "I have not failed. I've just found a thousand ways that won't work." This mindset is the key to transforming failure into success.

Why You Must Embrace Failure

You must be surprised by reading the heading but the truth is that failure is the key that helps you to garner experience and pave your way to working on a success mission. So how does failure help if you welcome it with open arms?

- **Failure Teaches Lessons Success Cannot:** When we fail, we are forced to analyse what went wrong. It is in this reflection that the greatest lessons are learned. Success often blinds us to the smaller details while failure forces us to look closer.

- **Failure Builds Resilience:** Every time you fall and get up, you become a little stronger. The act of rising from failure builds resilience which is the foundation of long-term success.

- **Failure Fuels Growth:** The discomfort that failure brings is often the very thing that drives us to improve. It forces us to rethink strategies, improve skills and work harder.

- **Failure Creates Opportunity:** Sometimes, what feels like failure is just a redirection toward a better opportunity. Doors that close might seem like a loss at first but they often lead to new paths you hadn't considered.

How to Embrace Failure

Is welcoming failure easy? Absolutely not. However, you cannot reach the other side of the calm land unless you face the storm. Here are some approaches to help you in embracing failure:

- Shift Your Mindset: Failure as Feedback

  The most effective way to embrace failure is to change how you perceive it. Instead of seeing failure as an end, view it as feedback. It's not saying, "You can't do this," but rather, "This approach didn't work, try another."

Ask yourself

- What can I learn from this?

- What adjustments can I make?

- Where did I go wrong?

- How can I improve?

By seeing failure as information rather than defeat, you empower yourself to grow.

- Own Your Failures: No Excuses

  One of the most powerful things you can do is take full responsibility for your failures. When you blame others or external circumstances, you give away your power. But when you own your failures, you take control of the narrative and open yourself up to growth.

- Take Accountability: Say, "Yes, I failed and here's what I'm going to do about it."

This isn't about self-criticism; it's about self-awareness. By acknowledging your role in the outcome, you put yourself in a position to make changes and succeed next time.

- Get Comfortable with Discomfort: Growth Lives Here

Failure is uncomfortable—it shakes our confidence and makes us question our abilities. But discomfort is where true growth happens. The more you lean into discomfort, the less power it has over you.

Accept the struggle. Understand that the road to success is paved with moments of discomfort and challenge. Those who thrive are the ones who accept this reality and keep moving forward.

The truth is, no one ever achieved greatness by staying within their comfort zone. Growth requires risk and with risk comes the possibility of failure.

- Persevere: Keep Moving Forward

Resilience is born out of persistence. When you fail, the worst thing you can do is stop trying. Failure is not final unless you let it be. Every successful person has a history of failures but what sets them apart is their refusal to quit.

Stay in the game. The only way to truly fail is to give up. As long as you keep pushing forward, failure is just a temporary setback.

Remember that success is not a straight line—it's a winding path filled with ups and downs. What matters is your ability to keep moving forward, learning and adjusting as you go.

The Power of Perseverance

Let's take a moment to reflect on a well-known story of failure and resilience—J.K. Rowling. Before becoming one of the world's most successful authors, she was a single mother living on welfare, struggling to make ends meet. Her manuscript for Harry Potter was rejected by 12 publishers before it was finally accepted. Had she given up after the first rejection—or even the tenth—the world would never have known the magical world she created.

Her story is a powerful reminder that failure is often a precursor to success. Those who succeed are not necessarily the most talented or the most fortunate—they are the ones who refuse to give up.

Action Steps: Turning Failure into Fuel

1. Start Small

If the fear of failure has been holding you back, begin by taking small risks. Set minor goals and get comfortable with the possibility of not succeeding. The more you practise, the less intimidating failure becomes.

2. Analyse and Adjust

After each failure, take time to reflect. Write down what went wrong, what you learned and how you'll adjust your approach. Treat it like a science experiment—failure is just data for your next attempt.

3. Surround Yourself with Positivity

Failure can feel isolating so it's important to surround yourself with people who lift you up. Seek out mentors, friends or communities that encourage resilience and growth.

Embracing failure is about recognising that it is not a reflection of your worth or potential—it is simply part of the process. It is through failure that you gain the wisdom, resilience and strength to succeed. Each setback is an opportunity to rise, stronger and more determined than before.

In the battle of you vs you, your biggest opponent isn't failure—it's the fear of failure. Overcome that fear, embrace failure as a teacher and you'll unlock a future filled with possibilities.

Remember, it's not how many times you fall, but how many times you get up. Success isn't about avoiding failure; it's about accepting it, learning from it and rising because of it. Now, go out there, embrace failure and let it be the fuel that powers your journey to success.

"Our greatest glory is not in never falling, but in rising every time we fall."

~ **Confucius**

25

The Art of Adaptability

"When we are no longer able to change the situation, we are challenged to change ourselves."

~ Viktor Frankl

In the fast-paced and ever-changing landscape of life, adaptability is not just a valuable trait; it is an essential skill for thriving in a world full of uncertainties.

Adaptability is the ability to adjust to new conditions, navigate challenges and embrace change with a positive mindset. It involves being open to new experiences, flexible in your approach and willing to adjust your strategies as circumstances evolve. Here's why adaptability is a crucial skill in today's world:

Embracing Change

Change is constant in life. From personal transitions to shifts in the workplace, being adaptable allows you to embrace change rather than resist it. This openness leads to growth and new opportunities.

1. Resilience in the Face of Adversity

Life will invariably present obstacles. Those who are adaptable are better equipped to bounce back from setbacks. They can pivot when faced with challenges, transforming potential failures into valuable lessons.

2. Enhanced Problem-Solving Skills

Adaptability fosters creativity and resourcefulness. When you encounter a problem, being adaptable encourages you to explore alternative solutions and think outside the box.

The Mindset of Adaptability

1. Openness to Learning

Embrace a lifelong learning approach. View challenges as opportunities to acquire new skills and knowledge. This mindset fosters growth and enables you to adapt to diverse situations.

1. Emotional Intelligence

Cultivate self-awareness and empathy. Understand your emotions and those of others.

2. Positive Attitude

Maintain a positive outlook even in the face of adversity. A positive attitude enhances your resilience and helps you remain open to new possibilities.

3. Focus on Solutions, Not Problems

Train yourself to shift your focus from problems to solutions. This proactive approach encourages a constructive mindset, enabling you to identify actionable steps when challenges arise.

Strategies for Cultivating Adaptability

1. Accept Change Gradually

Start by introducing small changes in your daily routine. This could be as simple as taking a different route to work or trying a new hobby. Gradually stepping out of your comfort zone makes you more comfortable with change over time.

Example: If you usually stick to the same workout routine, try incorporating different exercises or sports. This not only keeps your routine fresh but also challenges your body in new ways.

2. Practice Mindfulness

Mindfulness helps you stay present and centred amid change. Regular mindfulness practices such as meditation or deep breathing, enhance your awareness and emotional regulation.

Example: Set aside a few minutes each day to practise mindfulness. Focus on your breath and observe your thoughts without judgement. This practice helps you develop a calm and adaptable mindset.

3. Set Flexible Goals

While it's essential to set goals, flexibility in achieving them is equally important.

Example: If your goal is to advance in your career, be open to exploring various roles or responsibilities that may arise, even if they differ from your initial plan.

4. Develop Problem-Solving Skills

Strengthen your ability to think critically and creatively.

When faced with a challenge, brainstorm multiple solutions rather than fixating on a single approach.

Example: If you encounter a setback in a project, take a moment to list alternative strategies. This exercise encourages flexible thinking and boosts your problem-solving capabilities.

Let's read about Agastya's journey of adaptability

Agastya stood at the threshold of adulthood when life dealt its first blow—his father, backbone of the family, passed away unexpectedly. The grief was overwhelming but the practical demands of life soon took over. With the family's primary source of income gone, Agastya found himself facing responsibilities he had never anticipated. Bills piled up, and soon, he and his mother had to leave the home they had cherished for years. Homelessness loomed like a dark cloud.

With no option but to start over, Agastya took a job in a distant city. Packing whatever little he had, he moved to a place where he knew no one—armed with only his grit and a heart full of hope. As he stepped off the bus into the unfamiliar city streets, the weight of uncertainty pressed down on him, yet something within kept him moving forward.

At first, life in the new city was a whirlwind of challenges. The job was gruelling and the people around him were indifferent, focused on their own struggles. Agastya often felt like an outsider, a mere speck in a world that was far too big and far too fast for him to catch up. There were days when he questioned if he had made the right decision—days when he missed the familiar comforts of home, his father's reassuring presence and the sense of belonging he had once taken for granted.

Yet, in the midst of this chaos, Agastya began to realise something profound. Life wasn't about waiting for things to return to what they once were—it was about adapting, changing and finding strength in the face of adversity. He learned that growth often came from discomfort, and that sometimes, the very obstacles that seemed to block his path were the ones pushing him forward.

"When life breaks you, it also gives you the tools to rebuild."

Over time, Agastya built resilience. He faced each challenge head-on, learning to deal with people from all walks of life. In the workplace, he developed skills that not only earned him respect but also set him apart. Outside of work, he found solace in the simple things—taking evening walks, reading and reflecting on how far he had come.

He no longer saw his struggles as something to be endured but as stepping stones to a greater purpose. Losing his father had been a wound that left him scarred but it also taught him how to stand on his own. Becoming homeless had been a harsh reality but it also showed him the importance of perseverance and the value of every small victory.

As months turned into years, Agastya's hard work began to pay off. He moved into a small apartment, a far cry from his previous life but a testament to his ability to adapt and thrive. He made friends, found a support system and even began mentoring others who were going through similar struggles. The city, once unfamiliar and daunting, had become a place of opportunity, growth and transformation.

Agastya learned that life's unpredictability was inevitable but it was how he responded to it that mattered. He had lost much, but in that loss, he had found strength, resilience and a deeper understanding of himself.

In the end, Agastya's journey was not about reaching a destination but about learning to navigate the ever-changing tides of life. His story became a testament to the power of adaptability, showing that no matter how many times life knocks you down, there is always a way to rise—stronger, wiser and more determined than ever.

Agastya's life was far from easy but it was a life lived with purpose. His journey taught him that resilience isn't about being unbreakable; it's about finding the courage to rebuild every time you fall.

Agastya had learned to bend without breaking, and through his journey of adaptability, he proved that no matter how unpredictable life may be, we always have the power to shape our own path forward.

"In the end, it's not the circumstances that define you, but your ability to adapt and rise from them."

26

Celebrating Progress and Small Triumphs

"Success is a series of small wins."

In the journey of self-growth and transformation, we often focus so intensely on the final destination that we forget to pause and appreciate how far we've come. We set lofty goals, face internal and external challenges, and push ourselves forward—but what happens in between those milestones?

Every day, you wrestle with your own doubts, fears, habits and limiting beliefs. While conquering these battles can seem overwhelming, it's crucial to remember that every little win counts. The journey of self-mastery is built on incremental steps. Celebrating your progress isn't just a feel-good moment; it's a critical part of maintaining momentum and sustaining motivation. This chapter is about recognising and celebrating the small victories along the way because real progress isn't just about reaching the end—it's about the person you become through the process. How to celebrate progress meaningfully, in ways that fuel your growth and keep you focused on the next steps.

Celebrating progress matters because it:

- **Builds Confidence:** Every small win reinforces the belief that you are capable of change. When you acknowledge your progress, you build self-trust, which makes tackling bigger challenges less daunting.

- **Sustains Motivation:** Progress is energising. When you take time to celebrate how far you've come, you tap into a well of motivation that drives you forward. It reminds you that your efforts are paying off, making it easier to stay committed.

- **Shifts Focus from Perfection to Growth:** The aim isn't to be perfect but to grow. Celebrating progress helps you embrace the journey rather than obsessing over flawless execution. It reminds you that improvement—no matter how gradual—is the real goal.

- **Rewires Your Brain for Success:** You train your brain to recognise effort as a precursor to success. This shift in perception transforms challenges into opportunities, creating a mental landscape where growth becomes not only possible but inevitable.

How to Celebrate Progress Effectively

1. Track and Acknowledge Every Step

Keep a journal where you document your daily efforts, breakthroughs and even setbacks. Tracking your progress helps you visualise how far you've come and provides an opportunity to reflect on your journey.

2. Reward Yourself Mindfully

Create meaningful rewards that reflect your hard work.

It doesn't have to be extravagant; a simple reward could be taking a day off, enjoying a favourite meal or buying yourself something.

3. Share Your Wins

Sometimes, celebrating progress becomes more meaningful when you share it with others. Let trusted friends, family or mentors know about your achievements and create positive reinforcement from your support system.

4. Take Time to Reflect

Reflection is one of the most powerful ways to celebrate progress. Find a quiet moment to reflect on your journey so far.

Ask yourself:

- What have I learned?

- How have I grown?

- What challenges have I overcome?

5. Use Positive Affirmations

As you achieve small victories, reinforce them with positive affirmations. Statements like: "I am making progress every day" or "I am capable of achieving my goals" help you reframe your mindset. Affirmations not only acknowledge your achievements but also strengthen your belief in yourself as you move forward.

6. Celebrate the Process, Not Just the Outcome

A common pitfall is waiting to celebrate until the big goal is achieved. Instead, celebrate the process itself. Recognise the discipline it takes to wake up early and exercise, the perseverance needed to work through a difficult phase or the courage required to step outside your comfort zone. Celebrating the process keeps you focused on growth rather than perfection.

Progress Over Perfection

It's easy to feel like the battles you face are endless. But the truth is, the most important victories are often the small, quiet ones. Celebrating your progress is not about indulgence—it's about recognition, growth and honouring the hard work you put into your journey.

Remember, you are not just working toward a distant finish line; you are building a stronger, more resilient version of yourself with every step you take. Every time you celebrate progress, you reinforce the belief that you are capable of overcoming your inner battles. So take the time to pause and acknowledge your efforts. After all, the journey isn't just about who you're becoming; it's about appreciating the progress you're making along the way.

As you close this journey, remember: the greatest battles you face are within. Every challenge, every setback, is an opportunity to discover your strength, resilience and limitless potential. The power to shape your life lies in your hands. It's not the world that defines you but the courage you carry to redefine yourself with every step. You are capable of greatness, and the path ahead is yours to create. Never forget—you are unstoppable.

THE NEW YOU—Wise. Stronger. Unstoppable.